Writing
Aerobics I
Exercises for the Beginning Writer

Writing
Aerobics I
Exercises for the Beginning Writer

C.L. Sterling
and
M.G. Davidson

Northwest Publishing, Inc.
Salt Lake City, Utah

Writing Aerobics I

For information address: Northwest Publishing, Inc.
6906 South 300 West, Salt Lake City, Utah 84047
JC 10.9.95 / CR

PRINTING HISTORY
First Printing 1996

ISBN: 0-7610-0197-2

NPI books are published by Northwest Publishing, Incorporated,
6906 South 300 West, Salt Lake City, Utah 84047.
The name "NPI" and the "NPI" logo are trademarks belonging to
Northwest Publishing, Incorporated.

PRINTED IN THE UNITED STATES OF AMERICA.
10 9 8 7 6 5 4 3 2 1

To every client and student
who has taken to heart my advice on writing.
Cynthia Sterling

To my mother, without whose help
I would not be writing today.
Megan Davidson

Acknowledgment

Patrick Freeman, co-worker, editor and friend, whose insight and assistance on this book have been of great benefit to us. Thanks, Patrick, for your support. Like a true lion you have been brave, tenacious and at times, even a little cuddly.

Contents

Introduction

You have made the decision to become a writer. But what exactly does that mean? What is a writer anyway? Is a writer simply one who writes?

To be a writer, a marketable one, you've got to be good. That means you must know your craft and you must work at it continually to keep your edge in today's highly competitive publishing industry.

Wanting to write without learning the craft is like wanting to run a marathon without undergoing any training. Chances are you'll fail to accomplish your dream after the first few minutes or so. Logically, to realize a dream, goals must be set.

The marathon runner did not just wake up one sunny, crisp morning and decide to run twenty-six miles. It took a lot of sweat and yes, pain, to build up his endurance. It took hours of practice to establish a form and rhythm to make his running look effortless. So it is with writing.

Writing Aerobics I: Exercises for Beginning Writers should be viewed as a low impact, fat-burning introduction to the craft of writing. This book is not intended to qualify you to run the marathon, but rather to prepare you for the heavy-duty, back-breaking work that will follow.

After the introductory section, *Writing Aerobics I* is divided into two sections: The Workout: The Elements and Form and Technique: The Conventions. The Workout covers the most basic Elements of fiction writing, such as characters, plot, setting and tone/voice, and provides exercises for these basic building blocks of the novel. Without the foundation provided by these Elements, it is almost impossible to write what anyone would recognize as a novel. If the basic elements are handled poorly, then the writer will generally end up with a novel no one wants to read.

The second section of the book, Form and Technique, deals with the writing Conventions. These are specific techniques which a writer uses to create or enhance character and plot, the two major Elements. Conventions include point of view, flash-backs, plotting devices, scene and narrative and dialogue. Advanced exercises on point of view, theme, humor, writing difficult-to-render character types and other more challenging skills and topics appear in *Writing Aerobics II: Exercises for the Intermediate Writer.*

Before you get started, take a few deep breaths, raise your hands, reach for the stars and picture yourself where you want to be: a successful author who doesn't need a day job. The tools are before you, the goals are mapped out, the destination is known. Enjoy the workout.

Part I
The Warm Up

I like work; it fascinates me. I can sit and look at it for hours.

—Jerome K. Jerome

The workout room is before you. The computer, the paper, the desk and your own chair are waiting to be used. You've made the commitment. You've psyched yourself up. You are going to just do it. And this time you really mean it. You switch on the computer, put your fingers on the keyboard and suddenly you freeze with fear. Who are you trying to fool? You have no experience as a fiction writer. You are having difficulty typing the first word. How will you ever get a novel written?

Entering into any situation "cold" is not only uncomfortable but could prove harmful. Even the most skilled athlete knows the value of "stretching exercises" before beginning the workout.

It is no different for a writer. You have to limber up the fingers, put the brain in gear, and get the creative juices flowing before you can get to the serious business of crafting your novel. This should be done gently and without much effort. The following exercises were designed to stretch your muscles and make your heart beat a little faster. The sweating will come later.

1
Loosening Up: Freewriting

*A man may write at any time, if he will set himself
doggedly to it.*

—Samuel Johnson

Loosen up through Freewriting

Freewriting is the pre-writing activity which allows you to
express yourself on any topic, in any fashion, without deadlines,
restrictions, grammar considerations, or limitations of any kind.
The purpose of freewriting is to take away the fear that is

3

associated with the critical eye of a reader, publisher or editor. What you write is for you and you only. In freewriting you simply write whatever springs to mind. Once you've started writing, keep writing until you feel that your creative muscles are nice and loose and you're warmed up for the real work that lies ahead.

What Do I Have to Write About?

Virtually anything you want to write about will do. This is a no-holds barred warm up. But don't give the topic too much thought. If you think too much, you talk yourself out of getting started. Your goal is not to produce a polished piece, but to attain literary liberation. If you haven't found anything to write about, any one of the following exercises will get you started. Once you have chosen a topic, sit down in front of your computer and make yourself comfortable. Place your fingers on the keyboard. Now write whatever pops into your mind. Let the words tumble out onto the screen. Allow yourself to be carried away with the tapping sound of the keys. See yourself as a wild bird which goes where it pleases, starting and stopping at will. This freedom gives you a tremendous feeling of power—you are in control. The words belong to you, they are at your command, they come easily and quickly. You're beginning to feel good about yourself and your ability to release your thoughts in the form of the written word.

Stretching exercises such as freewriting should be done, if only for a few minutes, by most writers regardless of their experience or expertise. The following exercises, since they are so personal and are not meant to be read by anyone other than the author, do not include examples. There is no right or wrong way to do these exercise. So enjoy.

Freewriting Exercise One

Objective: To get started with freewriting

Go into your kitchen and select an object strictly on impulse. A spoon, a can-opener, a microwave oven, a blender, a clock, a wall plaque, a napkin ring—it does not matter what you choose, but choose something quickly. Examine it very carefully by looking at it, touching it, and, if feasible, listening to it. Now get back to the workout room and write whatever you wish, for as long as you desire. The only requirement is that you give at least some kind of reference to the chosen item. If you choose a spoon, for example, you might freewrite about your grandmother's spoon collection, your theories on the invention of the spoon, the way spoons look and feel, the material used in spoons, your child's first spoon, your souvenir spoon from Stockholm...anything goes.

Freewriting Exercise Two

Objective: To get started with freewriting

Remember the nursery rhymes you learned as a child? Hey Diddle Diddle…Three Men in a Tub…Baa Baa Black Sheep? They really didn't make a whole lot of sense then or now but they were fun to say out loud. Think of the nursery rhymes, songs, poems and stories of your youth, then write them down. Quickly. Don't worry if they bump into each other and get all tangled up. If the black sheep ends up in the tub in Mary Contrary's garden while Robinson Crusoe and Jack and Jill search for the Wizard of Oz in Neverland, so much the better. Keep going in this way as long as you can, splicing rhymes, lyrics and riddles.

You may have some fun patching together a lot of silly images and nonsense, but this exercise does have a legitimate purpose: You'll do a little harmless exploring with words and meaning, taking risks as you combine elements you would never otherwise try to combine. Much of novel writing involves seeking interesting combinations of ideas. This includes breathing a little new life into Dead-On-Arrival clichés.

Freewriting Exercise Three

Objective: To get started with freewriting

Freewriting may or may not tell a story, but in most cases freewriting concentrates on descriptions. Let's see what happens if you try to freewrite an event.

The following is an old grade-school exercise for writing a story, but it is an effective way to get the creative juices flowing. Choose a magazine and stop at the first picture you find particularly interesting or colorful, then write a paragraph or so about it. Afterward, see if there's a story you can tell about the figures or the setting in the picture. Does the picture show children washing a dog? Is it their dog? What would happen if the dog ran away? Is the picture of a man and woman kissing? Are they married to each other...or are their spouses in the next room, innocently watching TV? What would happen if the electric power went out?

Whatever story comes to your mind about the picture you've chosen, write it down. For that matter, write down as many story possibilities as you can think of. Do not worry about grammar or whether the ideas make sense. The goal is not "picture perfect" writing, rather that you have fun playing with the words and the meanings of those words.

Freewriting Exercise Four

Objective: To get started with freewriting

Keep a freewriting journal. This is a very effective way to build up your wind and increase your creative flow and keep focused and committed to your dream. It doesn't matter what you write or how much you write; half the battle is won by just disciplining yourself to write on a daily basis. Writing when the mood strikes you will not get you ready for the big race. There will be days, and plenty of them, when you simply don't feel like working the writing muscles. You'll have your share of days when you feel the pain more than usual. You are not alone. Even the most successful writers feel this way, but they don't give in to the headaches, the bad weather, or their mood swings. You will find, just like the runner, that you will hit a point in your workout where you reach the "writer's high." The sheer joy of the creative force running through you sweeps away any fear, pain, or hesitation. You actually become one with the words. It's a glorious feeling and one worth working for.

2

The Nonwriting Warm Up:
Freethinking

*"There is only one trait which marks a writer. He
is always watching."*

—Morley Callaghan

Freethinking, or observing, is something that you can do
anytime, anywhere. A particularly good place to practice your
powers of observation is in a crowd—a shopping mall, a busy
street, a park. As a writer you must be able to depend upon your
powers of observation to render effectively in your writing how
things smell, taste, feel and sound as well as look. Noticing

9

physical detail not only adds to your descriptive writing but can be used to reveal people's moods and personalities. The training of your powers of observation can be done as a mental exercise, or can be written down, either as you are out observing details, or later in the convenience of your home.

Observation Exercise One

Objective: To develop your powers of observation

Visual 1

Whenever you're in a crowd of people, such as in a shopping mall, choose a person that you see sitting quietly in the food court sipping his or her coffee. Study that person for a full minute. After your time is up, turn away and recall as many details about the person as you can remember: hair color, eye color, type and color of complexion, clothing, expression, position of body, arms and legs and so on. You only have three minutes, so be quick about it. Check yourself to see what you remembered and what you neglected or forgot. Remember, be discreet in your observations. The person should never know you're even watching.

Visual 2

Colors play an important role in providing details in fiction. With that in mind, while you're at the mall, choose a store window or any other setting and think about the many colors that you are seeing. Just don't see them, experience them; capture their shades, their essence. Notice nuances in shades. Brown, for example, might be chocolate, mahogany, chestnut, coffee, caramel, tan, beige, parchment, honey-brown, bronze or copper, plus many more.

Observation Exercise Two

Objective: To develop your powers of observation

Auditory

Capturing sound in a novel adds dimension to your writing. Learning to render sound is difficult and will take practice. First ask yourself, how skilled are you at observing and recording sound? To find out, keep a sound journal for a couple of days. Record the sounds you hear from morning to evening. The catch in this exercise is that you're not to write what the source of that sound is. If you hear the sound of a lawnmower, a woodpecker, a dog, a thunderstorm, or radio static, write the word or words that describe the sound. For example, the lawnmower might be roaring or purring; the woodpecker drilling, pecking or tapping; the dog barking, howling, growling, whining, yapping, yipping or squealing; the storm, rumbling, cracking, or drumming; the static crackling or snapping. Remember, do not name the source. Give only the sound. The next morning pick up your journal and try to identify the source of each sound.

Observation Exercise Three

Objective: To develop your powers of observation

Feel, Taste, Touch

    This exercise is best suited for the privacy of your home. The object of the exercise is to help you concentrate on your other senses, to help you observe, remember and write about objects. Choose a nice ripe piece of fruit, a container of yogurt or a piece of fattening chocolate cake. Touch it with your fingers—you can even gently roll or spread it over your hands or face. Feel it. Observe the texture, the coolness, the softness. Now smell it. Give it a good sniff. How does this smell affect you? Does the chocolate cake remind you of your grandmother's house, the apple of an autumn day, the yogurt of many diets you've been on? Finally, taste the food. Is it hot, cold, sweet, fresh? Does the taste remind you of other tastes? What memory is being triggered?

Cool Down

You're pumped up. You've just finished your warm-up exercises and you're feeling good. You realize that you can and do accomplish the goals you set for yourself. You now understand that through practice and repetition your skills will grow stronger. As you grow more confident you discover that you do indeed have much to offer. Now on to the workout.

Part II
The Workout: Elements

True ease in writing comes from art, not chance
As those move easiest who have learned to dance.
'Tis not enough no harshness gives offense,
The sound must seem an echo to the sense.

—Alexander Pope

Many people sit down to write a novel without the slightest idea of what a novel is. A novel is far more than 70–100,000 words on paper; it is, in its most conventional and basic sense, a structure or format. The Elements of the novel which are being addressed in this section are: characters, plot, setting, and tone/voice (theme is discussed in Writing Aerobics II). These Elements are the basic cornerstones of conventional fiction, and it is hard to craft a successful novel without using these important pieces.

Before getting started with the upcoming exercises, you may wish to start a file folder for your written exercises. These writing samples will provide an excellent record of how much your writing has improved with practice and learning.

Also, keep in mind that there is no right or wrong in writing; there is only what works and what doesn't. Most of the exercises in this book can be successfully completed in many different ways. There's no perfect solution to any of these exercises, so don't try and search for one. However, as mentioned in the introduction, if the Elements are not handled skillfully, chances are you'll end up with a novel no one wants to read.

3
Pumping Up: Character

Character is a victory, not a gift.

—Anonymous

Just as physical exercise will build up your body, the following writing exercises will pump up your characters. While fun and entertaining, these exercises should also prove to be hard work. Don't be surprised if you sweat a little. Just keep your mind focused on the goal. After the workout, treat yourself to something good. You deserve it.

The heart of the structure of a novel is the main character, or protagonist. Since the novel is essentially a story about someone, characters are the most basic of the basics of fiction writing.

Characters come in many shapes and sizes. Besides protagonists, there are antagonists (villains), major characters, secondary characters, and tertiary—or minor or ancillary—characters.

Since novels are about characters in conflict, and to a large degree the character drives the plot forward, it is paramount that the writer know everything there is to know about his character's background and psychological make-up.

The writer must see his character as a "whole" before he can effectively, and fully, render him to the reader. The creation of a believable and seemingly three-dimensional character doesn't just happen; you must work hard to build him.

After uncovering this vital information, the writer must then understand what is important for the reader to know, and learn how to weave pertinent information into the forward action of the story. Basically, the character's thoughts, feelings and actions speak louder to the reader than all the background information in the world.

Developing a Protagonist

Before you start to outline the plot of your novel in your mind or on paper, take some time to think about your protagonist. This is the character who will react to events in the story and ultimately be most affected or changed by them. Huckleberry Finn, Holden Caulfield, Bigger Thomas, Scarlett O'Hara, Tom Joad, and Jake Barnes are just a few of the more well-known protagonists in American literature.

The protagonist is the character whom your readers are

most likely to identify with. This character—man, woman, child or even an animal—is usually present for the entire novel, and his personality grows and changes throughout the novel. Without the protagonist, the novel would not exist.

A protagonist is dynamic and sympathetic.

A dynamic character changes and develops over the course of the novel, reacting to and responding to events in the novel. Because the events in the novel change his life, he is not the same person he was at the beginning of the novel. For example, a selfish young man forced to take care of his ailing grandfather might learn many lessons about human dignity and worth that change his outlook on life. On the other hand, an optimistic mother might become bitter and devastated by the prolonged illness and death of her child. In Mark Twain's masterpiece, *Huckleberry Finn*, Huck's experiences with Jim, the runaway slave, change the young white man's notion of human decency, freedom and brotherhood. Such a dynamic character is much more realistic than a character whose actions and feelings are static, predictable and shallow.

When we say your protagonist should be sympathetic, we don't mean she has to be Mother Theresa. However, she should engender the readers' sympathy at least on some level, even if she is a serial killer or a child molester. The reader wants someone to root for, someone who is basically decent though imperfect. The reader will experience the novel vicariously through this character. The less sympathetic the protagonist, the harder it will be for the writer to make his readers care what happens to the protagonist.

One beginning writer created a protagonist who murdered a drug dealer in cold blood. Granted, the drug dealer was a vicious brute, but in letting the "good guy" kill the defenseless "bad guy" the writer lost all reader sympathy for his protagonist

and actually gained sympathy for the antagonist. Your protagonist need not be a paragon of virtue, but he must have some
endearing or admirable quality. In most cases (but not all!), he
will also be an ethical person, an "everyman" struggling to do the
right thing in the face of adversity.

   To help you decide how to create a protagonist, try creating
a few from scratch. For now, he or she will exist in a vacuum
without the cushion of a story. Nevertheless, the characters you
create in the following exercises will be so well drawn that they
could take on the key role in a novel.

Character Exercise One

Objective: To create a character

Part 1: Physical Features

You are sitting at your desk when you spy a lump of protoplasm between the empty candy wrapper and the half-filled coffee cup. The lump, as ugly as it may be, is your protagonist. It's there waiting for you to breathe life into it. It wants to become a person, with hopes, desires, dreams. You are its creator, its god, so to speak.

Is this lump male or female? Tall, exceptionally tall, middling, short, petite, dwarfish? Stout, obese, muscular? Gaunt, thin, svelte, willowy, lean, raw-boned, slender? Somewhere in the middle? How old is the lump? What race or ethnic heritage?

The lump is now beginning to take form right in front of you. Let's say you've created a middle-aged Caucasian man with a fairly athletic physique, perhaps with slight love-handles and the beginnings of a receding hairline. Keep going, he's only partly baked. Keep molding and shaping him until he's standing on your desk, looking up at you in astonishment. What color are his eyes, his hair? Are his features soft or angular, rugged or patrician, or something in between? Is he a handsome gent, or would he be handsome if only his nose hadn't been broken in a brawl during his college days? Any other unusual characteristics? Was he a daredevil as a child? If so, perhaps he has a scar from his wilder escapades.

Part 2: Clothing

Once your protagonist is physically complete, you must clothe him (even if he is to spend an entire novel in the nude). What would this person wear? Dress him. Is he mild-mannered and conservative? A businessman by nature? How about a nice blue suit? If he's aggressive and conservative, give him a power tie and an unusual ring. If he's a conservative on vacation, you'll need to think about a polo shirt and Dockers. Perhaps he's in the military; then a suitable uniform is in order. Or is he the artistic type, the black turtleneck sort, the kind of fellow who'd wear an art director's tie? Perhaps he's rather radical, a rabble-rouser, an activist. Would he wear a sportscoat and torn jeans? Black leather accessories? A Grateful Dead T-shirt? Jeans and a flannel shirt? This last choice might also do for a rugged, outdoorsy type, or a cowboy or environmentalist.

Make sure you've given your creation, socks, shoes, underwear...even jewelry.

Does your new buddy need a hat? If so, what sort of hat? A Stetson, fedora, Irish walking cap, baseball cap, hard hat or helmet?

See him now fully dressed, looking good and feeling comfortable. As he's standing there busily checking out his new duds, ask yourself why he would choose to wear those particular clothes. Make sure your choice suits his personality and his professional status.

Part 3: Surroundings

Your lump is completely dressed. Now what do you do with him? You can't leave him standing on the desk between the candy wrapper and the coffee cup. He's looking at you, and his eyes seem to ask, Where do I belong?

Where a character lives or what he surrounds himself with will tell you a lot about his personality. Place him in the bedroom in his home. Is he a very neat, by-the-numbers kind of guy? Or is he a pleasant semi-slob who leaves wet towels in the middle of the floor? Does he have a few crazy, wild-looking ties tucked away in his closet?

Next, take him into the bathroom. Does he leave the lid up on the toilet so his dog can get a cool drink? Now, move to the living room. Does he collect fine art or beer cans? Is there a chess set in the corner of the room?

Take your character through every room in his house. Be sure to envision as many of his possessions as you can and allow the character to inhabit the space you have created for him.

Part 4: Background History

Now that your character has taken on a physical form and is feeling comfortable, it's time to have a conversation with him about his family, the town he grew up in, the schools he attended. What were his parents like? Are they still living? How does he feel about them? Is he proud of them? Is he having problems with his father? If so, what are they? How many brothers and sisters does he have? Are they a close family? Has one of the siblings drifted away from the family? What religion was he brought up in? Does he still practice it? What kind of job did his father have? Did his mother work?

Whatever question pops into your mind, ask it and he'll answer you. Once you have gathered all the information you require, you may decide to alter your character's physical features, choice of clothing and/or surroundings. That's the great thing about creating—you have the right to change or alter whatever you dream up.

Part 5: Psychological Profile

At this point, you should be very intimate with your character. It's time to ask him some more personal and probing questions. These questions are extremely important to the understanding of your creation: What are his desires? What are his motivations? If you understand those two things, you will know your character very well. You'll understand why your character made the choices that he made. You'll know why he opts to collect beer cans instead of fine art. You may discover that he wouldn't collect either one. Therefore, you must change his surroundings once more. You'll know why he keeps his loud, crazy ties hidden in the closet. You'll know why he chose to have a dog around in the first place.

If you do not know your character's motives and desires, you really don't know him at all.

Character Exercise Two

Objective: To create another character of the opposite gender

Despite what some people say, men and women are very different in the way they view life, and as a novelist you will probably need to create realistic male and female characters of a variety of ages. Try to avoid writing stereotypical "men" or "women" or characters who are "all bad" or "all good." Most people are a little of each.

The kind of visualizing exercise you've just gone through is very effective as a first step in imagining the potential in all kinds of main characters.

For this exercise, we want you to repeat the steps you took in Character Exercise One, this time creating a character of the opposite sex from the protagonist you envisioned in the previous exercise. You may wish to change the character's race, ethnicity, religion or whatever pleases you.

Naming a Character

Choosing a name is an important aspect of character building. A character's name often has a deeper meaning than merely a name. For example, Ebeneezer Scrooge could not have been a more appropriate name. Surely Dickens did not find that name in a phonebook. He put some thought into it, and the name became synonymous with every cheapskate who ever lived.

A name suits a character because somehow it reflects the sort of person he is. Holden Caulfield, the 15-year-old misfit in *The Catcher in the Rye*, suits his name precisely because it is very much unlike what most people consider a name. It doesn't fit in anywhere, just as he fails to conform to any level of society. Holden is also "holding in" his feelings and is very much "held back" by his and others' expectations of his actions. He allows himself self-esteem and respect only when he is in his rye "field" saving people's lives.

While the names you give your characters need not be fraught with such overt symbolism, the name should be appropriate for the character, and to some extent, suggest the personality of that character.

Character Exercise Three

Objective: To brainstorm character names

This exercise is simple and fun. Get an old magazine. Cut out ten pictures of people. Do not select the picture of anyone you know, including historical figures, contemporary actors, singers or politicians. A writer creates characters; he doesn't rehash them.

Once that is done, write one sentence describing the nature of the person and/or the job he holds. Now name each person.

Example:

The Picture: A thin, balding, middle-aged man clutching a briefcase.

The Description: The uptight CPA who just learned his wife has left him and drained their bank account.

Name: Matt Downer

Smashing Stereotypes

The most common problem among beginning writers is their use of stock or type characters. This is especially true among writers of action/adventure, fantasy, science fiction and romance where there is a strong urge to create a plot, then "plug in" a character so flat, so familiar, so clichéd that we swear we have seen him in a thousand TV movies. In fact, we probably have. That is one reason we strongly advise writers to avoid watching movies or TV shows while they are working on a writing project. These flat characters spring fully-formed from the writer's "mental image" of characters and roles he has seen or read before.

Some examples of stock fictional characters are:

> The Gruff Old Person Who is Really an Old Softy
> The Bully Who Runs When Real Danger Threatens
> The Coward Who Comes Through When the Chips Are Down
> The Noble but Misunderstood Member of an Other Race or Ethnic Group
> The Jealous, Vindictive Woman
> The Ruthless, Heartless Boss (Husband or Commander)
> The Cub Reporter
> The Mad or Nutty Scientist
> The Absent-Minded Professor
> The Rabid Liberal
> The Ultra-Conservative
> The Die-Hard Environmentalist

We don't need to know what these characters are like; they're already a part of our collective consciousness, and we immediately know what to expect of them. We also know that they are static characters who will not grow or change realistically during the course of a novel. The Coward becomes heroic without any reason or motivation, but simply because he has to change in order for the story to resolve and conclude. All these characters are much better defined by their role in a story than they are as individuals with varying life experiences and personalities based on those experiences. Of course, real people are not defined by their jobs or their station in life, but by their traits, their morals, their personalities and their social/environmental backgrounds.

Your job as a writer is therefore to invent realistic, interesting, intriguing characters. The following exercise is geared to help you expand and perhaps shatter stereotyped images.

Character Exercise Four

Objective: To smash stereotypes

Part 1

Write a short vignette on one or all of the following characters who are the opposite of what the clichéd characters usually represent. As you write, consider what events shaped the characters' personalities and helped them reach their present situations. How do these contrasts offer possibilities of change? How do these characters demonstrate their personalities?

1. An old-west sheriff who is a serious academic.
2. A prostitute who is independently wealthy and does not especially enjoy sex.
3. An African American civil rights activist who, perhaps secretly, is fascinated with English history and civilization.
4. The rich snob whose closest friend is a homeless person.

Part 2

Now that you've smashed the above-mentioned stereotypes, create your own list of characters who go against type. Write a short vignette on any or all of the characters you create.

Example:

Here's a character sketch of a general-issue character—the crusty old woodsman—with a twist:

Herman has lived alone in the Cascade Mountains for twenty years, ever since his wife's death. He knows every kind of tree, flower, animal and mineral that's to be found there.

People aren't to his liking, and although he often guides tourists and fishermen through the woods, he's a curmudgeon and doesn't do much socializing. When he does say something, he's likely to be caustic, sarcastic or melancholy, although, when pressed by adversity, he has a heart of gold and will go through hell and back to help a friend. He loves the mountains, hates politicians, and is wary of environmentalists.

Herman spends his free time oil painting. Since he is quiet and solitary, he expresses his feelings, hopes, dreams and fears through his art. He doesn't paint for money, although his paintings are beautiful. He has a degree in fine arts from a prestigious university, but he doesn't flaunt it. Whenever he experiences difficulty in his life, instead of turning to the whisky bottle, he turns to his easel. His acquaintances wonder about the man: He's a contradiction in terms, gruff on the exterior, but obviously a sensitive soul.

Character Drives Plot

Exposing five different characters to the same event will result in five different stories. Why? Because each person is unique, each character will physically and emotionally react to or think about the event in a different way. For instance, an older woman recently discharged from the hospital, a submissive child and a young man recently returned from military service will react very differently if someone curses at them.

The way your characters react to a given event will depend on many factors, including their age, sex, education, cultural or ethnic background and religion. Beyond that, their mental state and even their personal history play roles in the way they respond to events.

Imagine two people who are deliberately pushed by a punk on the sidewalk. Each person has the same physical reaction to the incident: Each confronts the young punk. However, each may have differing emotions about the incident and different reasons for being on the defensive. Character A has a macho attitude and feels that the push was an assault on his manhood. Character B feels angry at being assaulted. She has just ended an abusive relationship and has sworn to herself not to take any more abuse from anyone. Each of these characters has a different background. The same incident arouses different mental responses, and each character will have a different story to tell. Perhaps Character A will end up with a broken nose, while Character B, who has the courage of her convictions, will successfully drive away her assailant.

Notice that the event in question—a punk pushing a person—is secondary in importance to the reaction of the characters themselves. It is the personality of the characters and their thoughts and feelings which make the incident important. Something will happen (a fistfight or a personal triumph) because of the nature of the character, not because of the push, which is merely a catalyst for further events.

This is what we mean when we say, "Character drives plot," or "Plot development hinges on character development."

Character Exercise Five

Objective: To show how different characters react differently to the same event

Three different people experiencing the same event will tell you three different stories. Write a short piece for each of the following three characters: a football star, a thirty-year-old woman with a baby and a newly retired, sixty-five-year-old man. The situation is the same for each of them: Your character is walking through the park and comes upon a person being mugged. What happens next?

Here are some questions to consider before you write:

1. Will all these characters have the same reaction to the mugging? Why not?
2. The football star and the retiree may both want to help the victim, but will they both be able to? What might be their motives for going to the victim's rescue?
3. What is special about the woman's situation? What might be her motive for trying to help? Her motive for fleeing?
4. Which of these characters is most likely to be hurt? To scare off the mugger? To fetch help? To cower in fear?
5. What different opportunities for stories exist here, based on which character views the mugging? Have any of these characters been mugged before? Have any of them lost a loved one in a crime?
6. Might the economic and/or cultural background of the three characters be of importance to their stories? If so, in what ways?

Thoughts, Reactions and Feelings

To successfully develop a main character you must reveal the character's personality. This is done in two ways: 1) by showing us his actions and physical responses to situations, and 2) by showing us the character's feelings and thoughts, his hopes, his dreams, his fears and imaginings.

In the first case, you show your character physically responding to an event, i.e., diving into icy waters to rescue a child, or running away, or running to get help, or watching in fascination as the child drowns. The reader will certainly get a very visceral idea of what that character is like.

In the second case, you can take the reader into the mind of your protagonist and show us what he is thinking or feeling. This can be done by revealing his direct thoughts: *I'm terrified*, he thought…or by narrating his thoughts more indirectly: He took one look at the child and knew that fear had paralyzed him. (For more information on direct/indirect thoughts, turn to the chapter on dialogue.)

To understand your protagonist's thoughts and feelings, ask yourself what sort of person he is. What arouses his interest? What does he "want to be when he grows up?" What did he think lurked under his bed at night when he was a child? Whenever a barking dog approaches, how does he react emotionally?

What motivates your character to take action? Is it a fear of appearing "different" from other people, a desire to boost self-esteem by gathering wealth and accumulating "things," or the desire to right injustice and support the underdog?

Letting the reader know what your main character is thinking or feeling will tell us a lot about his values and ethics. For example, both a faithful husband and an unfaithful one may gaze lustfully at a beautiful woman at a party, but their thoughts will reveal two different stories:

Mr. True: *What a gorgeous woman! I'd love to get her in bed! Maybe I can find that sexy dress she's wearing in Linda's size and get it for her for her birthday. It would look great on her!*

Mr. Stray: *What a gorgeous woman! I'd love to get her in bed! I wonder if I can start up a conversation with her and get her phone number. If I play my cards right, I might land her. Laura is visiting her mother next week, so I ought to be able to work out the logistics.*

Notice how more powerful it is to reveal the thoughts of your protagonist rather than simply tell the reader "Mr. True ogled the woman but would never dream of cheating on his wife," or "Mr. Stray ogled the woman, plotting how he could arrange a tryst with her." Each character's thoughts, reactions and feelings help to define his character.

Character Exercise Six

Objective: To show a character's thoughts, reactions and feelings

Part 1

This exercise is designed to get you to concentrate on a character's emotional and mental response to an incident. The character is not permitted to react physically (at least not until Part 2), although her thoughts and emotions may lead to a physiological response (clenching teeth, shaking hands, balling hands into a fist, etc.).

Your character is shopping in a gift store at the local mall. It isn't very busy. Suddenly she hears a child crying. She turns to find a woman shaking a child and calling the child "stupid." The woman then slaps the child. The character knows the woman. It is her nice, loving next-door neighbor. The character is startled, and before she can make a decision on whether or not to confront the next-door neighbor, the woman has dragged the child out of the store. What thoughts and emotions run through the character's mind? What does the character imagine she will say or do the next time the character sees the next-door neighbor?

Write the scene.

Part 2

Later that same day, your character is out doing yardwork when the next-door neighbor stops to say hello. How does your character react now? What does the character say, if anything? Have your character's initial thoughts and feelings changed with the passing of a few hours? If so, how? How are these thoughts and feelings shown to the reader?

Write the scene.

The Frequent Cause of Conflict—The Antagonist

The antagonist of a novel is the antithesis of the protagonist. The antagonist works against the protagonist and tries to undermine the character's growth, development and success. This antagonism might also include trying to kill the protagonist or destroy his spirit. Because the antagonist tries to obstruct the protagonist at every turn, the antagonist is often key to the conflict in a novel. Many novels, including murder mysteries, action/adventure, fantasies, horror novels and westerns, are often a sort of dance between protagonist and antagonist in a fight between good and evil. The antagonist does not have to be inherently evil, however, but he is out to thwart the main character for one reason or another. An example of this type of antagonist is the lawman who is trying to track down the innocent hero who has escaped custody to try to prove his innocence.

This dichotomy between protagonist and antagonist is very clear in *The Lord of the Flies* by William Golding, in which a group of English schoolboys are stranded on a deserted island. One boy, Ralph, tries to maintain order and peace; another boy, Jack, appears to give in to the island's inherent savagery. The two boys work against each other and play off each other, each trying to disrupt the other's efforts, until the climax in which Jack and his minions try to hunt down and kill Ralph.

The antagonist builds conflict by setting up obstacles for the protagonist. Novels with strong antagonists usually feature a climactic scene in which the protagonist emerges victorious— the knight slays the evil sorcerer, the good cowboy plugs the twisted renegade, and the detective arrests the serial killer. In *The Lord of the Flies*, however, it is mere good fortune (in the form of adult rescuers) that prevents Ralph's death. In literary novels such as this, as opposed to genre novels, there is usually no clear cut "victory" for the protagonist over the antagonist.

Many excellent novels, especially literary novels, do not make use of traditional antagonists. In Steinbeck's *The Grapes of Wrath*, Salinger's *The Catcher in the Rye*, Conrad's *Lord Jim* and countless others, conflict arises from circumstances in the protagonist's life, events outside of his control or from facets of his own personality.

Character Exercise Seven

Objective: To create your own antagonists

Part 1: The Traditional Bad Guy

There has been another murder. It is the fourth murder with the same modus operandi. Your protagonist, an FBI agent, has been brought in to investigate. He immediately notices that all of the victims are born on June 5, 1975. Your job (and your protagonist's) is to do a character sketch on the killer (your antagonist). What are the killer's motivations?

Part 2: The Adversarial Bad Guy

In this case the antagonist is not necessarily a bad person, but he is put in an adversarial role opposite your protagonist. For example, write a character sketch on the antagonist for the following situation:

An efficiency expert is brought in to a company of free-thinking software designers to get the business to run more smoothly. Your protagonist is the most free-thinking, easy-going, non-linear designer of the bunch.

Part 3

Now that you've written a character sketch for "the traditional bad guy" and "the adversarial bad guy" according to our scenarios, it's time to create an antagonist of your own. Perhaps this character can appear in a novel of your own. Some things to consider: Is he a traditional bad guy or an adversarial bad guy? What are his motivations? His needs? His fears? Why does he have it in for the protagonist?

Secondary Characters

It is good to remember that not all of your characters will be major characters and that they certainly all can't be the star of the novel. Decide on your protagonist, then make sure he is the most prominent character in the novel and that it is his story.

Secondary characters are important. They may be your character's spouse, love interest, employer, child, mentor or best friend—or they may be a jealous lover, a psychopath or a vindictive colleague. They may be supporting your protagonist, or trying to "take him down." Whatever their role, secondary characters give dimension to a novel. They also aid plot by either siding with your protagonist or undermining his efforts.

An example of an effective secondary character is Bret, a tragic, beautiful woman in Ernest Hemingway's novel, *The Sun Also Rises*. Jake, the protagonist, loves Bret, but, because of a war wound, he is unable to make love to her. Hence their relationship is basically platonic. As loving but self-destructive Bret wanders from man to man, Jake is torn apart by wanting to "save" her and realizing he is powerless to do so. In this case, Bret is the focus of Jake's complicated sense of frustration and, on several levels, his impotence. She is not against Jake, but her thoughtless actions work against his well-being. Without Bret, Jake would be just another Angry Young Man beset by free-floating rage.

Some secondary characters, however, have minds of their own and are not resigned to playing second fiddle. It is almost frightening to observe how some secondary characters threaten to steal the action from the protagonist. You can't let that happen.

In one fantasy novel we reviewed recently, focus kept shifting from the protagonist, Pol, to his best friend, Ebo. When Pol should have taken action—impressed the enemy queen, shielded his emperor, tricked his enemy, captured dragons and so forth—Ebo seemed to push Pol aside and take over these duties himself. As a result, Pol became a peripheral character in his own story, while Ebo, who actually could have been deleted from the novel, stole most of Pol's thunder.

Secondary characters can be charming, colorful, attractive and important to the plot. They can even be necessary, like Bret, but they can never be the focus of the story. That is the role of the protagonist. Make sure your secondary characters know their place and don't let them run away with the story. As you will learn later, the best way to do this is to attach point of view to you protagonist.

Character Exercise Eight

Objective: To develop secondary characters

Good writing utilizes the personality traits of a secondary character by showing them through actions, details and dialogue. This two-part exercise has been designed to help you do just that.

Your character has been happily married for two years. Your character is honest and hardworking. This character is not well educated, but goes to night school in hopes of eventually earning an advanced degree in environmental engineering. The character's world is secure...until he meets an English teacher who makes obvious romantic advances at him.

Your character is both repulsed and intrigued.

Part 1

Write a short character sketch of the English teacher. What sort of person is she? Why is she pursuing the protagonist?

Part 2

Write a one- to two-page scene in which the teacher propositions the protagonist and he refuses her. Reveal only as much information from the character sketch above as is necessary to the scene. Remember, you should show the secondary character only through what the protagonist is able to observe about her.

Cool Down

You don't have a story without a protagonist. Once asked what his definition of a novel was, Graham Greene answered, "A novel is an unknown man, and I have to find him."

There are many ways to make your characters come alive. The kind of person your character is will be reflected in the way he behaves toward others. Therefore, it is essential that you know everything there is to know about your characters. Your character's personality is consistently being revealed through details and through his thoughts, actions, dialogue, emotions, fears, hopes, dreams, desires and motivations. The developing of a sound character is not accomplished through dumping exposition about his entire life in the first chapter or two; rather, his development is an ongoing process throughout the course of the novel.

This is particularly true of main characters and to a lesser extent holds true for colorful secondary characters.

4

The Workout Plan: The Plot

If one advances confidently in the directions of his dreams, and endeavors to live the life which he has imagined, he will meet with a success unexpected in common hours.

—Henry David Thoreau

When you are serious about getting yourself into shape, the best approach is to design a workout plan that best suits your needs. Routines, schedules and regimens help you keep track of your progress. Of course, you can alter them as your own needs change.

An organized approach is also of help when you plot a novel.

The following exercises will help you to identify the initial conflict, the rise and fall of action, and conflict resolution, as well as help you design ways to add conflict and suspense to your work. Sometimes a good plan is all you need.

While we stress that novels are character driven, we do not intend to undercut the vital role that plot plays in crafting a novel. Plot is a series of events that causes the main character and other characters to react, to take action or purposefully avoid taking action. The action the protagonist decides upon will cause him to become more and more embroiled in the action of the story and shape the events that follow.

For example, Claire, the protagonist in Diana Gabaldon's time-travel romance *Outlander*, is magically catapulted from 20th century Scotland to 18th century Scotland. When confronted with danger, she decides to marry a Highlander of that ancient period to help ensure her safety, although she is already married to a man in the future. Her decision, which seems like a good idea at the time and is clearly a matter of convenience, causes many complications when she falls in love with Jamie, her Highland husband, and decides to stay in the past with him.

The most important aspect of plot is conflict. This is the factor which will make the plot of a conventional novel go forward, building suspense for the reader and putting pressure on the protagonist. Conflict is basically an important question or troubling situation that pursues the protagonist during the course of the novel; in the end the protagonist must confront and resolve this conflict.

In *Outlander*, conflict arises partly from Claire's ambiguous feelings about being in a different time and culture, and partly from an antagonist who is bound and determined to destroy Jamie in body and spirit.

In a murder mystery, the conflict for a detective derives from the task of finding out who killed the victim and why. In a romance, the conflict could arise from a situation which threatens to keep two lovers apart, such as the family feud in *Romeo and Juliet.*

Conflict can take many forms. Matters of war, love, ethics, religion and physical dangers—such as being stranded on an island, like Robinson Crusoe—often ignite central conflicts for main characters. In *The Remains of the Day*, by Kazuo Ishiguro, Stevenson, a very proper British butler, finds that his growing attraction for an employee conflicts with his role as a household servant who always places duty and service before personal feelings. He is torn between love and his own identity. This conflict draws the reader ever closer into the butler's dilemma.

The Conflict Begins

Conflict is the force which drives your protagonist through the novel. If the protagonist is not in conflict with someone or something—if she is perfectly satisfied with the status quo and nothing happens to shake her out of it—then you are not likely to be able to craft a novel around her.

A character in a novel does not exist in a vacuum but is surrounded by and intimately involved in events. Most novels are driven by the protagonist's reactions to events. Something happens to the main character causing him to act and react. As a result the character changes for good, bad, or, in some cases, loses his opportunity to change.

An event which causes the character to react is called a compelling event. This first compelling event is used to catch the reader's attention and is sometimes called a "hook."

Plot Exercise One

Objective: To identify story hooks

Chose 3–4 of your favorite novels, either classics or books in specific genres. Try to identify the initial hook, or compelling event. This hook should occur in the first several pages or sometimes in the first several chapters, depending on the length and type of novel.

Here are the hooks in several popular contemporary novels. Note how many begin with an abrupt change in circumstance for the protagonist.

Examples:

> *The Firm* (John Grisham): A young lawyer is hired by a mysterious law firm that looks too good to be true.
>
> *The Shining* (Stephen King): A family goes to live in an old hotel with a strange, macabre history.
>
> *Lonesome Dove* (Larry McMurtry): Two veteran cowboys, fast friends, sign up as trail hands on a large, dangerous cattle drive.
>
> *Sphere* (Michael Crichton): A psychologist is asked to join a team of explorers investigating a sunken alien artifact.
>
> *H is for Homicide* (Sue Grafton): A young insurance investigator returns from out of town to discover that the police have cordoned off her office building to investigate the murder of her co-worker.

Plot Exercise Two

Objective: To put your character in an initial situation of conflict

Part 1

Your character is a hard working, ethical person who loves his job as a retail manager. He is married and has two younger children, ages six and nine. He has occasional money problems, but his spouse takes part-time jobs to help out. His dream is to save enough money to send his children to college, a luxury he was denied. Choose one of the four scenarios as the initial story hook. How does the character react to that situation?

1. The character comes upon his child, who has fallen from a tree. Blood is oozing from the child's head. The child is unconscious.
2. Your character has just learned that he has cancer.
3. The character has been arrested for embezzlement. The character is innocent.
4. Your character's numbers came up in the lottery. The ticket is worth six million. He has misplaced the ticket.

Part 2

If you have a protagonist in mind for a novel of your own, list the story hook and write the initial pages of your own book. If you don't have a novel in the works, create a few story hooks of your own. Who knows? Maybe one of these will stir up your imagination and launch you on a novel.

Rising Action

If you were to graph the plot of a conventional novel, it would appear as an upside-down check mark—rising gradually, peaking, then falling off abruptly. As the plot progresses, the action rises due to increased pressure on the character. This creates tension and suspense for the reader. This pressure builds to a point (the "peak" in the check mark) where the protagonist confronts the central conflict in the story and resolves it (or, in some cases, fails to resolve it).

The sequence of events plays an important role in the structure of a plot. If the sequence does not give an impression of rising action and increasing suspense or danger, the plot will appear to be disjointed and illogical—or, in other words, graphed like an upside-down question mark.

Benito Cereno, a novella by Herman Melville, is an excellent example of the classic use of rising action, also called "building action."

A British sea captain encounters a disabled ship populated chiefly by African slaves who claim that the crew was decimated by typhus. As the captain explores the ship and talks with the terrified skipper, Benito Cereno, he notices all is not as it appears to be. Disturbing clues cause the captain—and the reader—to doubt the slaves' story: Cereno is terrified of one of the slaves; a white sailor is wearing the remnants of an elegant shirt; some of the slaves start suddenly when the captain makes a sudden move; the figurehead is covered with a tarp. (The figurehead has been replaced by a human skeleton, a victim of cannibalism).

As the pressure mounts and the captain becomes more and more puzzled, the story reaches a climax when the captain at last realizes the truth: The ship has been overrun by the slaves. A skirmish ensues and the slaves are overpowered. A brief dénouement describes the subsequent trial and Cereno's death.

While the characters of the captain, the head slave and Benito Cereno are well drawn and compelling, the suspenseful plot line is at least as important to the effect of this story. The battle and dénouement are almost afterthoughts, because the conflict has been resolved the moment the captain understands the situation.

It is important for the beginning writer to realize that a novel is dynamic and must rise in action. A static novel, where nothing of great conflict happens, or an episodic novel, where incidents happen one after another in no particular order, will quickly fail to hold a reader's interest. Events must build upon one another, step upon step, until you reach the "peak" of the action, and the pressure is so great that the conflict must be resolved.

The following exercise has been designed to help you find ways to construct your plot so that the action rises in the story.

Plot Exercise Three

*Objective: To show how sequencing events affects conflict,
suspense and the rising action*

Part 1

Below are the key events in the plot of a simple, conventional western story featuring a hero named Josh and his
nemesis, Archer. As they appear here, the events are severely out
of order. They do not make sense, are not chronological and do
not logically build suspense. Rearrange these events so that they
create a conflict, build suspense and rise in action.

1. Someone fires at Josh from a house but he escapes.
2. Josh shoots Archer, disabling him.
3. Josh discovers that Archer, whom he sent to jail years
   ago for robbing a stagecoach, has been released from
   jail.
4. Through a clever trick, Josh leads the sheriff and a
   deputy, who are pursuing him, to Archer's hideout.
5. A guard is found murdered and the money he was
   guarding is gone.
6. Archer threatens the sheriff and deputy.
7. Incriminating evidence is found linking Josh to the
   guard's murder.
8. Josh rides into Sundance, a town he has not visited in
   years.
9. The sheriff discovers large amounts of money hidden in
   Archer's house.
10. Josh flees Sundance.

Part 2

Once the events are in order, choose two of the first five

events and write each up in a short scene, no more than two pages for each event. Do the same for two of the last five events on your list. The purpose of this exercise is to show how action rises from one scene to the next. Note that Josh does not appear in all of these scenes.

Part 3

Archer is not seriously wounded at his hideout and manages to escape. List some ways in which he might seek to take revenge on Josh, thus increasing the conflict in the plot.

Part 4

Now take your own novel idea. List some ways in which you can increase the conflict. Put them in a logical order so that you build suspense.

If you are not working on a novel of your own, use the story hooks you created in Plot Exercise Two and see if you can come up with a list of events that build upon your initial conflict. Make sure you order your events in a logical manner that causes the action to rise.

Conflict and Resolution

All good things must come to an end, even the plot of a novel. If the central conflict of the plot has been building throughout the piece, putting pressure on the protagonist to act and react, the conflict will reach its crescendo in the resolution.

Traditionally, fiction concludes when the conflict in the story is resolved. The protagonist dies...gets the girl...gets the job...wins the big race...fails and becomes a bum, and so on. Resolution is, classically, the release of tension caused by the central conflict that had built up during the course of the story. It is like removing a whistling kettle from a hot stove. Once the source of pressure is gone, the whole affair cools down and quickly reverts to a steady state.

Small conflicts may have separate resolutions. Many fine stories and novels end with unresolved conflict. Genre fiction, including horror, romance, action/adventure and fantasy novels, almost always end in resolution.

The climax, or high point of the rising action, is intimately connected with the resolution of the conflict, since the resolution of the conflict usually occurs in a climatic scene. The climax and the resolution are often followed by a scene or two of declining action, called the dénouement, in which the writer wraps up any loose threads and draws the novel to a finish, often with a reference to an event or image from the beginning.

Resolution of conflict often involves the death of the antagonist, or at least an act which renders him harmless to the principle characters. In Dickens' *Oliver Twist*, for example, the detestable but somewhat pathetic Fagin is hauled off to prison, while Bill Sykes, a more vicious antagonist, is killed.

Plot Exercise Four

Objective: To identify conflict and resolution

Using 3–4 classic or popular novels (not necessarily those used in Plot Exercise One), identify the central conflict and resolution, or climax, in each. What, if anything, do all these conflicts and resolutions have in common?
Examples:

> *Ethan Frome* (Edith Wharton): Ethan, Zenobia's husband, becomes entranced with her cousin, Mattie Silver, and she with him. They act on their decision to leave Ethan's domineering wife, only to become injured as they soar downhill on a sled during their escape. Mattie becomes an invalid totally dependent on Ethan and Zenobia's care.

> *Passage to India* (E.M. Forster): A young woman visiting India is overwhelmed as the exotic culture seems to strip away her sexual repression. Falsely accusing a Hindu doctor of rape, she is forced to confront her own weaknesses and prejudices on the witness stand.

> *Anna Karenina* (Leo Tolstoy): A woman abandons her husband and child for her dashing lover. When he grows bored with her and leaves her to go to war, she commits suicide by throwing herself under the wheels of his train.

> *Watership Down* (Richard Adams): Hazel, a rabbit, and his companions struggle to build a new warren after theirs is destroyed. They must

defend their new home against a monstrous "chief rabbit" and his hordes.

The Handmaid's Tale (Margaret Atwood): The protagonist, a "broodmare" in a futuristic totalitarian civilization, acts as a spy for an organization trying to overthrow the corrupt, misogynistic regime. Just as she is certain she is about to be arrested for subversive activities, she contacts an ally who promises to rescue her.

Plot Exercise Five

Objective: To bring the conflict to a resolution

In this exercise you will bring the conflict to a resolution. Sally (your protagonist) has been devoted to her fiancé, Jim, who was her childhood sweetheart. Jim has been missing in action for the past three years. She slowly allows herself to fall in love with Robert, an older man who is supportive and caring. Sally is about to agree to marry Robert when Jim arrives at her home. She learns that Jim was using the status of missing in action as a cover to go AWOL. He wants her to go away with him. The resolution of this story will come when Sally makes a decision between her two suitors.

Write the scene in which she makes her decision. Remember to show her internal reactions (thoughts and emotions) as well as her physical, external actions. Just as in *Benito Cereno* (when the conflict is resolved the moment the captain realizes the truth of what happened and not in the ensuing battle), the climax for this scenario may come at the moment Sally realizes what her decision will be; it may not necessarily be the moment at which she informs her suitors of her decision.

The Art of the Outline

An outline is one of a novelist's most useful tools. In an outline, the writer develops the novel's main characters by "sketching in" the compelling events which force the protagonist and other major characters to act and react. The outline is essentially a written graph of the rising action in the plot, beginning with the compelling event and ending with the conflict re   n and dénouement.

While most people think of an outline as something a writer creates at the very beginning stages of a novel, the information on what to include in an outline must be gathered over a period of time. Knowledge of how to create conflict, build rising action and craft a resolution and climax are crucial to drafting an outline.

Now that you have familiarized yourself with some of this information, you are ready to put together the outline of a novel of your own. You have studied the beginning, the middle and the end of a novel. You know how important chronological sequencing is to the logic of a novel. You realize that the development of the central character is key to creating a strong plot, and you are aware of the importance conflict plays in developing the personality of your protagonist.

An outline can be only a page or two long, hardly more than a sketch of the major events in the plot. On the other hand, it can be a long chapter-by-chapter outline which devotes a paragraph or two to each chapter of the novel. Many fall somewhere in between.

Outlines are extremely useful to a writer, since they offer a roadmap of the action of the novel. However, they should not be considered as the word of God. An outline offers direction, and is therefore flexible and changeable. A good writer will change his outline as he proceeds, whenever he thinks it is necessary. At some point he may even stop following the outline, because the characters have become so "alive" to him that he merely follows their lead.

One should never try to force characters to go through an event simply because it is on the outline. If characters seem to be resisting an event, examine the possible reasons. It could be that an action is out of character for your protagonist, or is unreasonable given the existing circumstances. For example, if your protagonist is a very nurturing person—or even just a decent, honest, loving person—you could hardly expect her to kill someone, even in self-defense, without feeling great remorse.

The following is an example of an unwritten woman-in-peril novel set in post-WWII England. NOTE: The numbers do not refer to chapters, but simply to the order of events.

Sample Outline: A Link With Sarah
1. Sarah Osbourne, a nurse in London during WWII, is caring for children injured in the Blitz. She receives a letter from her husband, Derek, a radio operator on the front lines. Sarah reminisces briefly about their life together, which so far has been childless.
2. Sarah is assigned to care for Benjamin, a badly injured boy of eight who recently arrived from a concentration camp. He is terrified of most people and exhibits some disturbing behavior, dismembering dolls and stuffed animals.

Slowly, Sarah begins to bond with the child. One day when she absentmindedly begins to sing a German lullaby her grandmother used to sing to her, he wails and thrashes in terror. She is horrified at what she has done.

3.   Sarah is devastated when she learns that Benjamin has been transferred to an orphanage while she was off duty. She desperately tries to locate him, but in the confusion of war time, his papers have been misfiled. When she is unable to find him., she throws herself into her work and tries to excise him from her thoughts, but she can't shake Benjamin from her heart.

4.   The war finally ends. Sarah is overjoyed when she is reunited with her husband. Sarah and Derek try to have children, but she learns that she is unable to have any. She tells Derek about Benjamin, and he agrees to help her find Benjamin so they may adopt him.

5.   Sarah and Derek try desperately to locate Benjamin. The hospital's records were destroyed in a fire. The officials don't remember one child's face amongst the many. She goes from orphanage to orphanage but is unable to locate Benjamin, whom she perceives as her lost child.

6.   The years of searching for Benjamin have proven to be fruitless. Her search comes to an end when Derek is incapacitated by a stroke. Sarah resigns herself to a lonely, childless life, sparked only by the time she must spend caring for Derek and volunteering at a local church.

7.   Benjamin shows up at her cottage, holding a letter she had written to one of the orphanages years ago. Sarah reaches out to him and Benjamin falls into her arms, crying. Sarah feels as

if at long last her child has returned. Benjamin becomes a part of her daily routine, and she feels as if her life has new meaning. Sarah's joy seems to affect Derek, who begins to show signs of recovery and regains some of his powers of speech and begins to walk with a cane.

8. Sarah learns of the gruesome dismemberment of a local minister. Later, she learns of a vicious attack on a businessman. The man eventually dies. After a third murder, local police suggest that this is the work of the same madman. Sarah is frightened that this could happen in her small town and starts carrying a gun for protection.

9. Benjamin is expected home for dinner, but does not arrive until the next morning. The previous evening a fourth murder occurs. When Derek questions Benjamin, he reacts violently, grabbing a plate and smashing it to the floor. Sarah remembers his reaction to her German lullaby and feels that Derek said something to trigger this reaction. She goes to Benjamin and comforts him, while Derek leaves the room angry.

10. Another murder occurs, but this time the victim lives long enough to give a description of the killer, which fits Benjamin. The police unlock a vital clue—all of the victims are former Nazi sympathizers or war criminals. Derek confronts Sarah with this information and proceeds to Benjamin's room in search of evidence. Sarah accuses him of petty jealousy. Derek finds a list of names and addresses, which includes the

name of the most recent murder victim. As he shows this to Sarah, Benjamin returns and overhears the conversation. Benjamin storms into the room, denying all wrongdoing and accusing Derek of lying to get rid of him. When Benjamin sees Sarah has doubts about him, he grabs Derek and threatens to kill him. Sarah pleads but to no avail. Derek tries to fend off Benjamin while Sarah searches for her gun. Benjamin has overpowered Derek and is about to deliver the killing blow with Derek's cane when Sarah shouts at him in German. Benjamin pauses long enough for Sarah to save Derek's life by shooting Benjamin in the heart. Sarah is glad that her first shot killed him, sparing her "wounded child" further pain.

11. Sarah and Derek visit Benjamin's grave. It is Tu bi'Shevat, the Jewish new year of trees, and she has brought a larch sapling to plant on his grave. Sarah and Derek both recite the Kaddish, the Jewish prayer for the dead, which they have learned for Benjamin's sake. Sarah feels she is also reciting the prayer for all the people killed in the Holocaust. Despite the horror of her experience, Sarah mourns for the "child" she has lost.

The above outline follows the classic lines of the novel: compelling event, development from that event, further events, rising action, pressure on protagonist, conflict and resolution, dénouement. Sarah, the protagonist, has gone through a difficult, character-building experience which has caused her to question her nurturing nature and gain greater appreciation of her own strengths, as well as her husband's love.

Plot Exercise Six

Objective: To write an outline for a novel

Okay, now it's your turn. Take some time to think through the plot of a novel and develop your characters. Choose any sort of long fiction—a literary novel or a genre novel. Make notes and character sketches if you wish, then write down the outline of the novel. You may follow the format in the preceding pages, or write a shorter form (similar to a synopsis) or write a chapter-by-chapter outline, normally the longest kind of outline.

Don't worry about getting something "wrong." After all, the purpose of this exercise is to practice writing an outline, not to perfect one. If parts of the outline seem awkward to you, rethink the structure of the outline and the actions and reactions of the characters. Are the events happening in a logical sequence that the reader can follow fairly easily? With the possible exception of the initial compelling event, do the events of the novel seem to flow naturally from the actions of the characters? Are the characters behaving in fairly realistic ways? Is the protagonist sympathetic?

If you feel up to it, come back to this exercise every time you feel you have a viable idea for a novel. Except for a few spots that are "under construction," can you outline the plot completely? If not, chances are your idea needs more work and your plot needs greater structuring. Perhaps the conflict needs to be stronger and the suspense more consistent throughout. Think in terms of applying pressure to your protagonist and letting your protagonist react to that pressure.

Cool Down

In summary, the beginning writer should always remember to structure the plot chronologically and logically. Establish the conflict quickly and allow your protagonist to react to it. The ramifications of his actions, as well as those of other characters, will heighten conflict and create a feeling of suspense, a sense of "rising action," as the reader wonders what will happen next. To some extent, the plot is the "peppermill" through which your protagonist must be ground before he can change, develop, and gain insight into the human condition.

An outline is an invaluable tool for the beginning writer, since it can provide him with a blueprint for where the novel is heading.

5
The Gym: Setting

> To write fiction, one needs a whole series of
> inspirations about people in an actual environ-
> ment, and then a whole lot of hard work on the
> basis of those inspirations.
>
> —Aldous Huxley

Novels, like real life, do not take place in a vacuum, nor do
they happen in environments which are devoid of time. Setting
is the term used to describe the place and time in which the
novel takes place. Of course, the writer may make use of several

different times and places in one piece. The trick is to make the reader feel as if he is in a given place, at a given time.

In general, novels begin with a character—often the protagonist—in a setting. This is because, if we are simply introduced to the character without a setting, we will have difficulty envisioning him separate from some sort of environment. In a very basic way, a protagonist is part of a place and time, even a product of a place and time. For instance, a child brought up in 18th century France would act differently from a child brought up in 20th century France or 18th century Virginia.

Let's take a look at the two aspects of setting—place and time—separately.

The Right Place

"Place" is a pretty large concept. North America is a place. So is the United States. So is the state of Oregon. So is the city of Portland, OR. So is the Crown Point Bank on the corner of Morrison and 12th in downtown Portland. So is an office within the bank…and so on.

To differentiate big, general places from small, specific places, we refer to the former as "broad" places and the latter as "narrow" places. "China" is broad; Beijing is more narrow, and a noodle shop along the riverfront of that great city is narrower still.

Broad places often require a lot of research. For instance, if you wish to set your novel in Newfoundland, you'd better know quite a bit about this Canadian province or be prepared to learn about it. On the other hand, if you are from Minnesota and your novel takes place in your home town, then you'll probably have all the information you need to create the setting "straight from the heart."

Narrow settings often require no research beyond that of a fairly active life. You have probably been in a fancy restaurant, a roller rink, a movie theater, a high school classroom, a farm building, a modest home, a swanky home, and on and on. Some narrow settings, however, especially exotic or foreign ones—that Chinese noodle shop, for example, or an open-air market in Calcutta—will no doubt require extra research.

Establishing Place Through Images

Now that you are aware of the importance of setting, the next thing you must consider is how to bring your setting to life. Sensory images are a very important tool for establishing a setting. We should not only see the setting, we should hear, touch, smell and possibly taste it as well. For instance, if the place is the beach of a tropical island, we will probably see the contrast between the sky and sea, the green of vegetation and the glint of the sun off the water. We will feel the warmth of the sun and the coolness of the water on our feet or the breeze from the ocean. We'll feel the grainy texture of the sand under our feet and the bubbles of the seafoam, and we'll hear the roar of the surf, the cry of seabirds and the islanders calling to each other in their native tongue. Perhaps we are sipping pineapple juice, or maybe it's planter's punch or something even stronger.

Of course, not all this imagery may be necessary. The idea is to create a setting so real that your reader can imagine that he is in that particular place, drinking in its atmosphere. The following exercises are designed to help you create a setting rich in atmosphere.

Setting Exercise One

Objective: To identify how Place is created

Read the first page or two of several of your favorite novels, either those you have used in these exercises before, or different ones. Pay attention to how each author establishes the setting of the novel. What sensory images does the author use to establish Place? In each case, does the setting tell you anything about the protagonist?

Setting Exercise Two

Objective: To establish Place

Everyone has a favorite place. It could be a "narrow place," such as a special table at a restaurant or a room in a specific house, or it could also be a "broad place," such as the island of Hawaii.

Write about your favorite place as if you were setting the first scene of your novel in that place. Write this exercise in the first person ("I"). What is striking or unusual about the place? What are the sights, sounds, textures, smell and tastes of the place?

Setting Exercise Three

Objective: To clearly establish Place within a scene

Part 1

It is important to let the reader know just where a specific scene is taking place.

Read the following:

> e next day Lisa noticed Jack when she looked up to hand Brad her keys. Jack walked up to Lisa and grabbed her by the elbow. "That's it," he said. "You're coming home. Now."
>
> Lisa broke away from him, glaring at him. She thought he had understood that it was over, that their relationship was history. "Go away, Jack. Don't you understand? We're finished. That's all there is to it. Come on, Brad, let's leave."
>
> Lisa felt her legs begin to tremble as Brad stepped between her and Jack. "Mister, leave the lady alone. She doesn't want to go anywhere with you."

Where is this scene taking place? What are the characters doing? Where are they in relationship to each other? Does the setting help to define the characters? We don't know, because we don't know where we are.

Part 2

Now rewrite this passage, setting it in a particular place. Things to consider: Where are Lisa, Brad and Jack? Is this a place they've been before? What time of day is it?

Character and Place

To some extent, Place impacts on characters and exerts some influence on them. A thirty-year-old American man, for instance, will feel and act differently in: the jungles of Viet Nam; a hospital; a concert hall; a tavern in Helena, Montana, or a Nepalese village on the way to Mount Everest. Will he be the same person in each setting? Yes and no. Although his basic personality will remain intact, he will have different reactions, expectations and emotional responses to each setting, and perhaps even memories of each.

Setting Exercise Four

Objective: To develop the relationship between Place and character

Part 1

Place helps define character. Here's the setting—now who is the character?

1. A shack in the swamps of the Louisiana bayou.
2. An old castle in Scotland.
3. A ghetto apartment building.
4. A moon station.
5. A recently remodeled farmhouse.

Part 2

Now that you've placed a character in each of the above settings, choose one and write a short scene, having the character interact with his environment. How is the setting established? What sensory images are used? How does the setting help define the character?

Setting Exercise Five

Objective: To show how different places affect character

A woman character whom you know relatively well is going on a blind date with a man whom she is to meet at a specific place. She has seen his picture, so she knows what he looks like.

Write a brief scene of 4–8 sentences in which these two characters meet for the first time in the following settings. Her blind date has chosen the place in which they are to meet. Be sure to include sensory descriptions. Note how each place influences the characters in specific ways, including dress, speech, emotions and reactions to each other.

1. A California fern bar
2. An amusement park
3. A bowling alley
4. A performance of the opera, *Madame Butterfly*

The Right Time

Time is just as much a part of setting as Place and has just as strong an effect on characters. Just as Place could be divided into broad and narrow categories, Time can be thought of in two different ways, period and chronology. Period refers to the historical era in which a novel takes place. Chronology refers to the sequence in which events take place.

Period

Historical/period novels must be rich in accurate details. For the historical/period writer it is imperative to get the period detail right. The possibilities for period settings are as vast as history itself—from the Roman Empire to the Revolutionary War to such relatively recent times as 1960s America—but the possibilities for errors are greatly increased as well. To illustrate that point, read the following passage:

> "General! General Grant! Sir! Sir! Urgent news, sir!"
>
> Avery rode into the camp at a gallop and reined up in a swirl of dust. The general, who was posing for a photograph with his officers, squinted in annoyance. Avery thought Grant looked as if a chigger had bitten him. "Lee is on the march, sir!"
>
> The officers swarmed around Avery as he dismounted, but the general stayed seated. He stared at Avery for a moment, then motioned him forward. "Boy, go fetch me my phone," he said.

If the anachronism of a telephone in early 1860's North America hit you like a punch to the stomach, then you can imagine what it feels like for a reader to come across a period detail that is wildly misplaced or blatantly inappropriate.

Inappropriate detail, most of the time, is not as outrageous as a telephone in the 1860's. More often than not, it appears as a bit of inappropriate dialogue, a historical sequence out of order, or some other faux pas that gives the impression that the writer did not do his research very thoroughly.

While Grant might say, "Okay," for instance, Christopher Columbus certainly would not. Civil war buffs would be immediately distrustful of any novel which has the Battle of Gettysburg taking place before the Battle of Shiloh. There is, however, some room for poetic license. For example, E.L. Doctorow in *Ragtime* let Harry Houdini meet with Woodrow Wilson. Not all readers notice or care about historical inaccuracies. For the discerning reader, however, an inaccurate period detail is like having cold water thrown on your face while sleeping—it immediately brings you out of a "dream state." Publishers are likely to be miffed by the writer who pokes too many holes in the fabric of history as well, especially if he is doing so because he has not done his homework.

A good point to keep in mind when writing historical/period novels is that many of the people who read these types of novels are looking to learn a little history in a sugar-coated fashion. So it is important to keep one's facts straight.

The most common and disconcerting error that writers of period fiction make is to place 20th century characters in period dress and assume that they have created characters indicative of another century. This simply is not so. The moral codes, ethics, values, mores and guiding principles of human civilization have changed from century to century, as well as from place to place.

It is folly to believe that a 19th century American woman would behave or think exactly like a 20th century American woman.

Attitudes about cursing, women, racism, illegitimacy, adultery, homosexuality, the penal system, disciplining children, duty to one's country and many other values-oriented topics would be far different from those of today. Some research, including reading pertinent non-fiction books about the values of a chosen time period, is in order for anyone wishing to write a period novel.

Contemporary novels must also be rich in accurate details. Too often the writer of contemporary fiction includes references to popular movies or fashion without realizing that in a few years these references will most likely be forgotten. Therefore, a contemporary fiction writer will want to avoid using detail which will soon become archaic or dated. The following exercises will help the contemporary fiction writer as well as the period/historical novelist with the development of setting.

Setting Exercise Six

Objective: To eliminate period inaccuracies

Part 1

Read the following scene set in the American Revolutionary War. Look for period inconsistencies. Some are obvious, some are more subtle.

> Elizabeth sat in the library, trying to compose a letter to her sister, Mildred. Just as her pen ran out of ink, she heard a noise at the door and in bounded Rex, her father's golden retriever. The dog slid over the linoleum floor and bumped against Elizabeth's bare leg.
>
> "Daddy!" cried Elizabeth as her father entered the room. "Did you speak to Tobias?" She caught her breath; even the mention of her beloved's name made her heart race.
>
> "Liza, I'm afraid I have some bad news for you, dear," said her father. His shoulders were hunched and his gray eyes, normally so bright, looked as dull as cardboard. "Tobias already has a wife."
>
> Liza took a sharp breath. So now her father knew as well. "It doesn't matter to me, Daddy," she said softly. "I shan't care if I ever get married. I've decided to visit him in Boston anyway."
>
> Her father nodded. "Perhaps that is best," he said. "You're a woman now, almost seventeen. You know your own mind better than anyone else. But be careful, daughter. I fear Tobias is not to be trusted."

Part 2

Rewrite this scene removing any modern references and replacing them with appropriate ones so that the reader will believe she is vicariously experiencing the scene. Some points to consider are: What items and terms seem out of place? What attitudes are being expressed toward adultery? the role of women? the role of parents and children? Do they seem appropriate for the time?

Setting Exercise Seven

Objective: To show the values of characters in a different period

It is 1890, in a small town in the midwest. A man is standing in the town square, screaming obscenities about his neighbor and closest rival. The man has been drinking, but he is not drunk.

Write a few sentences describing how each of the following people would react to the raging man. Keep the era in mind.

1. The sheriff
2. The schoolteacher
3. The man's wife
4. The man's rival
5. A boy of 10
6. The local minister

Chronology

Conventional novels are usually written in chronological order. This allows the reader to easily follow the events as they occur. Chronologically ordered events seem realistic and believable because they follow the time patterns of our daily lives. For example, we get up in the morning, eat breakfast, go to work, and so on. Days follow days and months follow months in natural progression.

While innovative novels are often not in chronological order of events, chronological order is the easiest, most effective tool for constructing the passage of time in a conventional novel.

Novels do not normally begin with the climax and resolution. The writer works his way toward a resolution, just as a person works his way through the day. This allows the writer to build suspense and slowly increase tension.

Closely aligned to the idea of chronological order is the concept of sequence. Events happen in a given order: The phone rings, you pick up the receiver, you say, "Hello?" The phone would not ring after you pick it up.

Nevertheless, many beginning writers often present an event in a very confusing sequence, something like this:

> I fell to the ground, bleeding from a gash in
> my lip.
> Henry had taken a swing at me and struck
> me square in the mouth, although I had tried to
> duck. I felt an impact, then pain.

Obviously, a person can't fall down from a blow he hasn't received yet. Nor can he exit his house and drive down a street without entering some sort of vehicle. Nor can he talk to a person he hasn't met yet and the reader does not even know is present. These observations may sound obvious, but it is amaz-

ing how many beginning writers have difficulty with chronological sequencing and end up needlessly confusing their readers.

Setting Exercise Eight

Objective: To put a scene in proper chronological order

Part 1

Read the following passage involving a blind date, keeping chronological order in mind.

Steven was supposed to pick her up at six that evening, so Liza spent the hour before then dressing and putting on her makeup. He had called her that morning and specified that she shouldn't get dressed up, but Liza rationalized that a silk shirt and long black harem pants weren't really dressy. She wondered what sort of restaurant he was taking her to.

She answered the door when she heard the doorbell ringing and stared out the doorway in confusion. There stood a tall, angular man in jeans, a flannel shirt, and, most peculiar of all, a black Stetson. "Liza? I'm Steven. Ready for the rodeo?" he asked, helping himself to a beer from the fridge.

Liza stared at him open-mouthed. "I'll…I'll have to change my clothes," she stammered. "I thought we were going out to eat." Steven had told her something about dinner, and she had assumed he had meant a restaurant. What sort of dinner could they get at a rodeo? Hot dogs? And why a rodeo? He hadn't told her anything about that, she was sure.

The night before, when Clara had told her about this guy Steven, Liza had been charmed by Clara's description. Clara had said he was tall, dark and handsome, but she had not said anything about cowboy gear. Now, Liza saw that Clara had been right in a way, because Steven was handsome, but he was not at all what she had expected.

Later, at the barbecue in the fairgrounds, Liza found herself enjoying the chicken, beans and corn on the cob when Steven laid his hand on her shoulder. "Time to go back to our seats," he said. "That rider I told you about drew Nightmare, and I just made a bet with a friend that he wouldn't go the full eight seconds."

Liza nodded and followed Steven back to the grandstands. The rider he had pointed out earlier was strutting about behind the chutes as if he owned every single bucking horse there. "You're right, he does look conceited," Liza said.

Part 2

Yow! Are things ever out of chronological order here! Rewrite the passage so that the timing is logical and the writing does not constantly shift backward and forward in time.

The Time Lapse

Normally when there is a shift in scene, there is a corresponding shift in setting or time. Even if the physical place has stayed the same, time has lapsed. There may be new characters in the new scene, or completely different characters.

For example, if the reader has just finished a scene set in a hospital with Sadie, a mother in labor, and her sister Rose, the reader will expect the same setting, time and characters as he continues reading—unless you tell or show him differently. Therefore, if you wish to follow the hospital scene with a scene one month later showing Sadie with her new baby and her husband Peter, you will have to establish the new setting. One way to do this is as follows:

> The doorbell rang, and the baby began to cry. Sadie hurried out of the kitchen into his nursery. She picked up Donny and held him close. He was so tiny and fragile, she scarcely believed that he was already a month old; it seemed as if he had just been born. "It's okay, honey," she soothed him, stroking his red, wrinkled face. Sadie patted his back and hummed to him as she listened to Peter's voice downstairs. He was talking to someone, obviously the person who had rung the doorbell, but Sadie did not recognize the nervous, high-pitched voice.

Failure to establish the lapse of time and a change of place is a common mistake among new writers. A space break between scenes often helps the reader realize a new scene (and a new time or setting) is taking place, but a space break alone is not enough to establish a lapse in time. Unless you are writing a military novel or the equivalent in science fiction, avoid using headlines to establish time and place (The American Embassy in Bonn, Germany, August 15, 1994). Headlines echo the style of a military log, and must be used appropriately.

What if physical setting stays the same but the time has progressed? Regardless of setting, time takes place in a novel the same way it takes place in real life, and it must pass in a realistic manner (with some exceptions in science fiction and fantasy).

Imagine a scene with the Whittaker family eating breakfast in their home. A subsequent scene set later in the day will show them eating dinner or preparing for bed. A scene set months later, but still at home, might reveal that a child has left for college, or that the family is preparing for their summer vacation or for a skiing trip, depending on the season. A scene set years later but still at home will show more significant changes in the characters and their family: the absence of children, alterations in financial status, and so on.

In general, try to avoid long time lapses between scenes. As more time elapses, it becomes increasingly difficult to bridge the gap between scenes and preserve a sense of chronological flow. Some sort of exposition, perhaps in the form of dialogue or flashbacks, will be necessary to bring the reader "up to speed" on what has happened during long periods of elapsed time.

Setting Exercise Nine

Objective: To establish the time lapse between two scenes

In the kitchen, at breakfast, Bill, with briefcase in hand, announces to Mary, his wife, that he is leaving her and the children. Later, Mary tells her children what has taken place.

Your job is to write these two scenes, clearly establishing the setting of the second scene. Where is it taking place? What time is it?

Cool Down

Remember that setting is composed of both time and place. The reader must get a feeling for where and when the action is taking place and which character is delivering the action. The setting is usually established right at the beginning of a scene, so readers can visualize where they are.

6
Toning Up: Tone and Voice

Words are all we have.

—Samuel Beckett

Tone and voice are two sides of the same coin, a coin called human emotions. If a writer writes without regard to his reader's emotions, the writing will sound flat and distant. If characters behave as if they have no feelings, they will appear to be made of cardboard, not flesh and blood people with dimension.

Tone

All people have feelings, including the writer and his readers. A writer can play on readers' feelings by appealing to their emotional nature.

How we feel about a given topic or situation is reflected in our language and our actions. For example, we shout, curse, mutter, grumble, and generally act and speak in an aggressive way when we are angry. We speak and act softly, gently and compassionately when we are sympathetic to others.

Writers often try to elicit certain feelings in readers through the use of language, and we refer to this aspect of writing as tone. Tone is not easy to create, since it generally arises naturally from the plot, characters, and writing style. It is something that is developed over time, with practice.

Flat writing is devoid of tone and is sometimes called scenic writing. Here's an example:

> Martin walked along the shore, picking up pebbles from time to time and skipping them across the top of the water. Alice, walking behind him, asked him to stop because his actions made her feel nervous. He complied and they continued up the beach, with Alice stopping now and then to pick up shells and bits of driftwood. "I'm sorry about Tom," she said at last.
>
> "You're sorry? I thought I knew you. Now what are we going to do? What am I going to do?"
>
> "I don't want to talk about it anymore," Alice said.
>
> She showed a shell to Martin, but he did not seem interested.

What's going on here between these two characters? What are they thinking and feeling? Alice seems to have had an affair, and Martin seems angry, but nobody's feelings are very clear. Because of the emphasis on physical movement, the passage has no emotional drive to it and little tension or drama. It is as if the scene is choreographed. The characters' words and actions do little to reveal their moods; hence, the tone is as flat as a pancake. There is no emotional information being conveyed, except perhaps the fact that the stone-throwing makes Alice feel nervous and Martin sounds upset. That's not very thorough, realistic or dramatic. The whole paragraph seems distant and cinematic. It fails to arouse our emotions.

If this were a movie, a director might add dark shadows, dramatic lighting and the haunting cries of gulls to add tension to the scene. But this isn't a movie. It's a passage from a novel about a husband and wife who are having marital difficulties. Here is the same passage, rewritten in a tone of veiled anger and sorrow. Here the writer is actively trying to solicit feelings from the reader. Notice the difference.

> Martin walked along the beach, picking up pebbles from time to time and skipping them over the gray, flat waters of the ocean. He threw each stone further and harder than the last, trying to throw some of his rage and frustration with them.
>
> "Hey, stop that!"
>
> He turned and saw Alice, her face half-hidden by a dark scowl. She padded so quietly behind him that he had forgotten she was there. "Why?"
>
> "It makes me nervous," she said, brushing a damp strand of blonde hair out of her eyes. She

looked a lot older than she had that morning, he thought, before she had told him about Tom. "I don't like it when the stones land on the water. It looks like the water is being broken. And besides, it scares the gulls. It's just scary, you know?"

"Well, it is a little scary around here now, isn't it? It's scary not knowing about us anymore, not knowing you like I thought I did."

She shook her head and bent to pick up a scallop shell the tide had left behind. "Let's not talk about it anymore, okay? We've talked enough. Look at this shell! Isn't it pretty?"

Martin frowned into her hand. In an instant he seized the shell and threw it into the ocean, where it bobbed once, then sank out of sight. "It was pretty, yes."

How does the writer add a feeling of anger, drama and sadness to this passage? For one thing, the choice of words is important; the ocean is gray and flat, Alice's face is dark, her hair damp and she looks old. Alice "pads" and Martin "seizes," words indicative of restraint or submission, and anger or power. The characters also reveal their moods by their words and actions, and sometimes we are aware of their thoughts. Martin throws the stones with rage and frustration; when he throws the shell, it is as if he is throwing away his marriage. Alice is worried about the gulls and scared by the thought of a "broken ocean," a concern which reflects her worry for her breaking marriage. She clearly tries to distract Martin from thoughts of her adultery with the shell. These words, images and actions pull at the reader's feelings, solicit an emotional response and create an overall feeling of despair.

Tone Exercise One

Objective: To recognize tone

To recognize tone, ask yourself what the writer is doing to elicit an emotional response from the reader. Is it word choice? Imagery? Actions that speak louder than words? Character dialogue, thoughts, or feelings? Do words or images build on each other to create a compelling picture of the character's life? Or is the writer merely giving us surface information: names, dates, activities, concrete observations?

Read the sentences below. Mark an "F" beside the ones that seem flat and devoid of tone; mark a "T" beside the ones written to elicit an emotional response.

1. Harry and David had been friends for many years, and they frequently got together to play cards and share a few laughs.
2. Once he knew where he was going, Bret folded the roadmap, tucked it into the glove compartment and eased the old Buick back out onto the highway.
3. Jessie shivered when she saw his face. Blood dripped from his mouth. Had he been in an accident…or a fight?
4. The stallion was a beautiful animal. His coat was pure black and his tail long and full. Robert was sure the horse would fetch a good price at the auction.
5. What a horse! The stallion looked even better than Robert remembered. His coat shone like black satin and his tail streamed out behind him when he ran, like a banner. *It's gonna break my heart to sell him*, Robert thought, *but I have to.*
6. Marie took the frog from Justin and cupped it in her hands. It wriggled against her palms, wet and slimy.

Little boys were disgusting brutes!

7. The mountains looked bright pink in the glow of the early morning sun.

8. The wind, like a mischievous child, batted the tops of the pines, sending a fine sugar-dusting of snow to the ground.

9. That day in April in 1066, and the Saxon army was in no shape to withstand the onslaught of the Norman fighting force. Harold, a fair-to-middling general, was taken off his guard and had no time to prepare a stand against William's well-equipped horde.

Tone Exercise Two

Objective: To add tone to a flat scene

Part 1

The following scene is an example of flat writing. Read the sample.

> Shortly after they were seated, Dan and Wendy ordered a magnificent dinner of crab legs, French onion soup and half a dozen whisky sours. Before they knew what was happening, they found themselves at a motel a few blocks away from the restaurant, checking in for the night. The night clerk thought they looked like a couple of honeymooners who couldn't wait to get into the sack. They were clinging to each other, kissing and rubbing each other all over. Dan even had a hard time getting in the elevator, because Wendy was pawing at him nonstop. The moment they entered their room, Wendy tore off Dan's shirt and jeans, and Dan shucked off her skirt and oversized blouse. Wendy clasped Dan around the middle and pushed him back onto the bed.

Part 2

Now rewrite the scene giving it tone. As written, it is virtually a direction from a movie script. It is extremely distant, cold and clinical, despite its sexy premise. About passion, it is nevertheless passionless. It is as if a reporter is in the bedroom, taking notes. We know these people are attracted to each other simply because of their physical movements and because the writer implies they have sex.

What sort of emotion can you add to this passage to make it more involving, more human, more moving? In other words, how can you give it tone? Here are some things to ask yourself:

1. In whose viewpoint is this interlude taking place, Dan's or Wendy's? In other words, who is observing and reflecting on the action?

2. What is Dan's and Wendy's relationship? Is it clandestine or not? Is this their first tryst or their tenth? Could they be a married couple?

3. What do they feel for each other? Do they each feel the same way about each other?

4. What sort of people are Dan and Wendy? Are they basically decent or not? Shouldn't we know something about their personalities?

5. How well do they know each other?

6. What might they say to each other?

7. What words might reveal their feelings?

8. Is the night clerk important here? Would you lose anything by getting rid of him?

Voice

If tone is the writer's attempt to affect the emotions of the reader, what is voice?

Voice also has to do with affecting the emotions, but the emotions involved with voice are those of the characters themselves. All people have feelings, even fictional people. Just like flesh and blood folks, fictional characters are affected by their emotions, and these emotions come out in the way they speak, act, and think. If their feelings mirror the situation they are in, then their response is appropriate.

For example, a father feels happy when he watches his child celebrating her eighth birthday at a party as she opens her presents and shares cake and other goodies with her friends. If the father is not happy—if he is angry, sullen, sad or distant—his voice, reflected in his words, thoughts and actions, will seem inappropriate. If there is a reason for his unusual reaction to his daughter's party, then readers will have to know why. Did he just lose his job? Is his wife leaving him? Did his daughter scream and curse at him moments before the first guest arrived? Certainly these facts will affect his reaction to his daughter and her party, but the reader must be aware of them.

Voice also mirrors the personality of a character. Strong protagonists often develop a unique, characteristic voice. Celie in *The Color Purple* by Alice Walker has a very strong, definite voice (or way of expressing her feelings in language), as does Holden Caulfield in J.D. Salinger's *The Catcher in the Rye*. Does your protagonist speak in a dialect? Does he like to tell stories? Does he always cut right to the heart of the matter? Does he have a large vocabulary (maybe he's an English professor), or is he uneducated, with a coarse, humble vocabulary? Does he wear his heart on his sleeve, or does he try to hide his feelings?

The kind of person your character is, the way he reacts and

the things he does will affect his voice—the way he expresses himself. This is especially important when a writer is creating a first person narrator, that is, a character who is telling his story directly to the reader. In such a work, the character's voice is one of the few tools the reader will have to help him understand the narrator's personality.

Voice Exercise One

Objective: To recognize voice

Match the passages to the character. Rely on the emotion expressed by the character (his voice) and the special aspects of his expression (also his voice) to tell who is whom. In most cases, these quotes are reactions to specific events. They are all in the first person. Character choices are on page 101.

1. I told the others not to worry, that I was just going down the path a ways to see what was to be seen. But of course, that wasn't the case completely. You can't be too careful on the trail, and if you get a feeling you ought to act on it.

2. I couldn't believe he'd do that to me. He might just as well have ripped my heart out and stepped on it. How could this man possibly have been someone I once trusted to the depth of my soul?

3. I remembered a story my grandfather told me once, the tale of a prince named Ossain and the Land of the Ever Young. Maybe it was too sad for children—the prince dies in the end—but I figured they were strong kids and could take it. It would show them that things aren't always what they seemed, and they'd need to learn that if they were ever going to have a prayer of getting on with their new "mom."

4. I told him no, no more. I wasn't listening no more. I wasn't letting him do this to me any more. I told him I knew I wasn't very smart. That was all right with me. And if I was everything else he said I was, that was all right too. But at least I was mine, whatever was left of me, and not his. How good it felt to say that to him!

5. This sort of thing's been happening to me for years now. You walk into a situation, everything appears clear-cut, obvious, I-know-just-what-happened. And then one little tiny thing will be out of place. An ashtray a little too close to the end of a table. A cat hair where there shouldn't be a cat hair. And everything you believed was happening isn't happening anymore, and you're back to square one because of some nothing detail you probably wouldn't have noticed if you were a normal person.

6. I found it difficult to believe that David didn't try to contact me immediately following Michael's accident. After all, I had instructed David to keep a watchful eye on Michael and let me know if anything untoward was happening. I believed David was a dependable sort, and I had impressed the urgency of the situation upon him.

7. It's always me, you know. My fault. The car doesn't have gas, then it must be because of me. I run short of cash and I get the blame. It's not like I'm the only one who drives the car, after all. And I've got a lot of expenses.

8. He and I got out of the car at the lounge. Everything would have been fine except I didn't like the way he looked at me. I don't know what it was about that look, except for a moment I didn't feel like I was a person anymore, and it was his look that made me feel that way.

9. Some of these guys, they try to weasel out on you. You do your best and you work hard and what do you get? A lie, the old run-around, or even a slap in the face. Basically none of these guys are any good, but at least you can reason with some of them. I don't let anyone take advantage of me.

10. The last time I saw her, she looked up at me and laughed. I don't recall her face very well, but I remember

her laugh very clearly, sharp and high, almost a gasp. She might as well have been saying, "You mean nothing to me anymore." I can't believe she's gone.

A. Betty, a grandmother who loves her grandchildren.
B. Lauren, a college co-ed.
C. Henry, a distinguished scientist.
D. Gabe, a man well-versed in the ways of the woods.
E. Pete, a detective at the scene of a murder.
F. Jay, a teenager.
G. Kelly, a veteran prostitute.
H. Susan, who had always been a dedicated wife.
I. Steve, suffering a bitter divorce.
J. Maria, who has reached her limit.

Voice Exercise Two

Objective: To add voice to a passage

Part 1

Read the following paragraph, written in the first person.

One Saturday morning I went downhill skiing with my boyfriend Jeremy. I had only been skiing once or twice before, and that was years ago. I wasn't very happy about going, but Jeremy told me I'd do fine, and I believed him. The slopes were fairly crowded, even though it was early. Some of the people were all dressed up, and some of them were like me, just wearing ordinary winter clothes. I rented some equipment and took a lesson, and Jeremy told me I was doing well enough to take the chair lift to the top of the mountain with him. I had neglected to tell him that I had never gotten off a chair lift before, and I didn't tell him on the way up the mountain until we were within a few yards of the little ramp where you're supposed to lean forward out of the chair and gracefully ski off the lift. When I told Jeremy I didn't know what to do, his mouth fell open and he stared at me. Then suddenly we were at the ramp. I lunged forward without thinking and began falling backward. The edge of the chair caught me in the back of the head, and I flew forward into the snow. I spent the rest of the morning in the Ski Patrol hut while Jeremy continued skiing.

Part 2

This paragraph is virtually voiceless. It is hard to tell much about the narrator's personality from this paragraph, as the language is flat and colorless, despite the dramatic situation. What sort of person is the narrator? We haven't the slightest idea.

Remaining in the first person, rewrite this paragraph using the voice of three of the following characters:

1. A snotty prima donna.
2. A teenage girl who has grown up in the inner city.
3. A sixty-year-old woman whose daughter keeps insisting that "she get out and get some exercise."
4. A fairly recently divorced, middle-aged woman.
5. A movie star traveling incognito.
6. Jeremy's mistress.

As you write, think about how the person's state of mind and feelings are going to influence her language and how she tells her story. If you're up to it, continue this exercise by retelling the story in the voice of the three characters you did not use before.

Voice Exercise Three

Objective: To write a passage with a strong voice

Choose any one of the characters from Voice Exercise Two (or another one that you know equally well) and use his or her voice to rewrite all of the following brief, flat passages. Give specific details whenever you can and don't be surprised if these snippets end up as much longer passages.

1. When I stepped into the deeper reaches of the forest, I could hear birds singing.
2. I remember Christmas time when I was a kid. We ate a lot of food and had a lot of fun.
3. The only time I ever tried to ride a horse I fell off and made a fool of myself.
4. My brother died two weeks ago. It was a nice funeral and my sister gave a moving eulogy. Still, I will miss him badly.
5. When I was in college, I was fond of acting and got a degree in drama. I couldn't make a living off it, though, so I got a job working in real estate. It was an okay job, a lot like drama.

Cool Down

In closing, think of tone and voice as places where the "heart" of the novel is visible. Both tone and voice are attached to the emotions: tone affects those of the reader, and voice reflects the emotions of the characters. Tone is frequently of importance in third person novels ("he/she"); voice is almost always a function of first person narration ("I") and omniscient narration ("the all-knowing narrator"). Be aware of the tone you are creating in your novel and make sure it is appropriate. Develop three-dimensional, colorful characters who will speak and think with their own unique voice, or style of expression, which is appropriate to their age, culture, sex and level of education.

Part III
The Conventions

Through the study of technique—not canoeing or logging or slinging hash—one learns the best, most efficient ways of making characters come alive, learns to know the difference between emotion and sentimentality, learns to discern, in the planning stages, the difference between the better dramatic action and the worse. It is this kind of knowledge…that leads to mastery. Mastery is not something that strikes in an instant, like a thunderbolt, but a gathering power that moves through time, like weather.

—John Gardner

By now you should start seeing the benefits of writing exercises. You're becoming disciplined, you feel better and your goal is within reach. But you've also realized that something is missing. Your movements are as full and as extended as they should be, but sometimes you "jerk" and "strain" during your writing workout. What is missing? The answer is form and technique. It simply is not good enough to go through the motions. You must learn the ways in which you can achieve maximum benefit from your writing exercises.

The following chapters cover such diverse topics as point of view, scene and narrative, dialogue and imagery. These literary conventions will help you to hone your skills for writing strong characters, enhancing plot, and setting the scene. As with any good exercise, the better the form, the more you will get out of your work. Enjoy.

7

Developing Form: Point of View

The great art of writing is the art of making people real to themselves with words.

—Logan Pearsall Smith

Nothing…nothing is more helpful to your understanding of fiction writing than a thorough knowledge of point of view (POV). Many beginning writers have difficulty understanding this important concept. It is as essential to your writing as character and plot, though many beginning writers have never even heard of it. With a thorough understanding of point of view and sufficient practice in using it, your writing will become more focused, more effective and more powerful.

Point of view in literature refers to a specific perspective or angle of observation from which a novel is narrated. A novel is basically a story; hence, someone is observing the events and characters in the story and reacting to them. This "someone" could be an omniscient narrator, but usually the POV character is the main character in the novel, the protagonist.

An event, in life or fiction, takes on different meanings to the different people involved in the event. Each person will have different feelings, and therefore a different perspective. This is the basic idea behind the concept of literary POV.

Say a twelve-year-old girl is caught shoplifting a sweater from a fashion boutique. The shopkeeper calls the child's mother and she hurries to the store. Each of the three people involved in this scenario will have a drastically different outlook on the situation. The girl is embarrassed and angry; her crime, which she conceived of as a whimsical prank or flirtation with danger or act of defiance, has backfired and probably cost her several allowances, as well as a certain amount of freedom. Plus, there is the public humiliation and her mother's scorn to deal with. The shopkeeper is concerned on two counts: one, he cannot afford to lose merchandise, so he is upset with the girl for treating his livelihood with such disdain. On the other hand, he realizes the child is very young; he wants to be generous and kind with her, as long as he can protect his own interests. The mother, though she is perhaps also embarrassed, is more concerned about her daughter's apparent lack of ethics than anything else. She may be thinking, Where did I go wrong? What can I do to help little Nicholette? To the mother, the incident is not simply a matter of right or wrong, but an indication of her personal failings as a parent.

It was one incident—but there were three different ways of looking at it. A bigger incident, such as a war, might elicit many different viewpoints, depending on the roles and personalities of the people involved in the war: the recruit who welcomes the chance to show his valor; the veteran who dreads the next battle, fearing it will be his last; the field doctor, overwhelmed with the sheer amount of death and suffering; the owner of the munitions factory, who views the war as a great financial blessing; the statesman, who welcomes the war as a challenge to further his career; the soldier's sweetheart, who fears for her lover's life and sees war as insanity; the journalist, at once distant observer and participant, who feels pressure to act like a professional, despite the emotional strain; and so on. Whoever first said, "There is more than one side to every story" was setting forth the basic premise of POV.

POV Exercise One

Objective: To write in different characters' Points of View

Part 1

Read the following passage, written from the point of view of Tad, a stable boy who has just been told that the racehorse he adores and has taken care of for two years is irreversibly lame.

> I said they couldn't give up on her. Ice Age was too good a horse. Doc wanted to put her down, but I said she deserved another chance, there must be something Doc could do. He shrugged. "She's in pain," he said. "Even if this disease didn't cripple her completely, the pain would be on and off. She'll never run again, that's clear. I say let her go."
>
> Mr. Schmidt, who owned Ice Age, ran his hand over her swollen leg. "Isn't there something you can give her?" he said. "You know…a painkiller? I've got a fortune in this horse. She's supposed to run in the Breeder's Cup next week."
>
> Doc shook his head. I knew what he was thinking: Lame horses dosed with painkillers usually ran themselves into shock until they fell and broke a leg. I patted Ice Age's neck and felt a tear run down my cheek. "You can't do that, Mr. Schmidt," I whispered.
>
> "Hell I can't!" he snapped. "She's my horse, and I say she runs."
>
> "Then get yourself another vet," said Doc, and he turned abruptly and strode out of the stable.

Schmidt frowned and spat into the straw. "Tad, go call Dr. Finster. He'll get this nag up and running," he said.

I stroked the mare's soft muzzle. I didn't want her to think that I had abandoned her. My eyes were so full of tears that everything was a blur, including Schmidt's red, angry face. I was so heartbroken, so enraged, so utterly devastated that nothing seemed to make sense anymore.

"Get yourself another boy," I told him. But I didn't walk from the stable. Once I got out of the stall, far enough away from Ice Age so I wouldn't spook her, I ran.

Part 2

Now write this passage from the point of view of Doc or Mr. Schmidt. How do they feel about Ice Age's situation? Consider the agenda of each man. Perhaps Doc has seen a lot of horses suffer with this disease. Perhaps Mr. Schmidt has a lot of debts or an illness in the family. How does each man feel about Tad and his reaction to the bad news?

Write your exercise in the first person—"I"—just like the sample.

Types of Points of View

There are two basic literary points of view, first person and third person. These are the viewpoints, or perspectives, from which most novels are told. Third person is of two basic kinds, attached and omniscient. A third kind of third person POV, called scenic and its cousin, cinematic POV, are not recommended for beginning writers, though we will discuss scenic and cinematic POVs in this chapter.

While there is no intrinsically bad POV, some POVs are easier to use than others, and some are better suited for certain types of novels.

Let's start by examining the first person POV. It is often mistakenly used by beginning writers, because it appears easiest to use. This is not the case. However, if handled carefully and purposefully, it can be a very effective form of narration.

First Person

In the first person, the novel is "told" to us by a narrator, the "I" of the story. This is Huck Finn in *Huckleberry Finn*, Holden Caulfield in *The Catcher in the Rye*, Lestat in Anne Rice's *The Vampire Lestat*, and Scout in Harper Lee's *To Kill a Mockingbird*. They all tell their story directly, as if they are talking to an audience or writing to a correspondent.

The first person creates a sense of intimacy and immediacy, making it a good choice for detective/mystery, romance, coming-of-age and some horror novels. It is also *the* POV for fictional reminiscences and many introspective literary novels.

A first person narration has an almost confessional or confidential feel to it, as if the narrator is telling you the reader (and you alone) some secret from his life. This POV greatly reduces the feeling of distance between the reader and the narrator. It is easy for the reader of a book written in the first person to imagine that he is part of the novel, there on the scene, listening to the narrator.

Protagonists are easy to develop in the first person, because the narrator, who is "speaking," is revealing all sorts of information about himself through his voice—his word choice, his sentence structure, his descriptive language, and what he chooses to reveal or keep hidden from "his audience." As you continue to explore first person, keep the concept of voice in mind. Remember that the narrator tends to reveal his personality in the way he expresses himself. First-time writers often choose to write in the first person because the narrator is so easy to develop and because it is so easy to stay in the narrator's POV.

But the first person has some drawbacks, too. For instance, some writers feel the urge to add other first person narrators in the same manuscript. Some writers develop a "first person pompous" style of narration, using overblown, bombastic language dripping with self-importance and self-absorption; this sometimes gives the narration an inappropriately "gothic" sound. ("What madness seizes me now and compels me to write down these torrid events?") Or the writer may lose control of his first person narrator, allowing that narrator to indulge in interior monologues—long, rambling accounts of personal reflections, opinions or memories. These usually have little or no bearing on the story and simply cause unnecessary digressions. In addition, it is very hard to describe the narrator in first person, since he is not likely to talk much about his own appearance. It is also difficult to find out what other characters are thinking, except through dialogue, and it is virtually impossible to render the death of the narrator in first person.

Keeping all these things in mind, let's explore the first person POV through the following exercises.

POV Exercise Two

Objective: To rewrite a third person passage in first person POV

Rewrite the passage below, currently in a rather flat third person POV, as if Mattie is directly telling us the story. Before you write, ask yourself what sort of person Mattie is. How would she tell this story? You will need to "get in her head" and understand her personality before you can express her feelings and reactions. Do you think it is best written in the first person or third person?

An extremely disturbing thing happened to Mattie the next day, when she took Timmy and Ricky to the Renaissance Fair in Agoura. While the boys were intently watching the antics of an acrobat juggling apples and a hatchet, Mattie saw a blonde woman threading her way through the crowd, a tall man at her side. Mattie wouldn't have looked twice except that the woman was so out of place among the casually-dressed tourists and the people in medieval garb. The blonde wore a short red sequined dress and matching red pumps with heels so high that the woman staggered over the rough ground. Her face was plastered in makeup, and her hair was done up in an elaborate bouffant. *She looks like a hooker,* Mattie thought, glancing at the boys. She hoped they didn't see the garish woman, but she herself was fascinated by her. Mattie looked back at the woman and saw that she had stopped at a food booth and was buying some sort of gooey confection. Just as Mattie decided she was being stupid to waste her time watching this bimbo, the tall man, who had had his back toward her, turned and looked in her direction.

It was Dave. They had only been separated for two weeks, but he hadn't lost any time "finding himself."

Mattie felt angry. She hurried over to the boys and hustled them away from the area, hoping they hadn't seen their father.

Some things to consider:

1. How would Mattie describe her disturbing feelings about the incident?
2. Think of how Mattie would feel about the woman in the red dress. Would Mattie simply say that the woman's skirt is "short?" Would she dismiss the woman's hair-style as "elaborate?"
3. Why do you think Mattie finds the woman fascinating? Would Mattie elaborate on the details of her fascination?
4. How would Mattie say she reacted to seeing Dave with the woman in the red dress? How would Mattie describe her anger? Would she imagine how the boys might feel if they saw their father with the woman?

POV Exercise Three

Objective: To practice writing in first person POV

Part 1

Choose a character whom you are familiar with. Keeping
that character's personality in mind, write a paragraph or two in
which he or she narrates the following scenes. (All scenes should
be in the past tense and the first person. Be careful to avoid an
overly-dramatic or gothic voice. Note that this exercise is not
necessarily based on detective or murder mystery fiction. Assume the narrator is addressing his audience/reader.)

1. He or she finds a dead body.
2. He (or she) relates the time his friend told him she had
    found a dead body.
3. He reads in the paper that police have found the body of
    his friend, who had been missing for weeks.
4. He meets a person whom he suspects has murdered his
    friend.

Part 2

Choose two of the scenes above and write them in the first
person point of view of the following:

1. A ten-year-old girl
2. A retired police chief
3. A woman who has just lost her husband to a debilitating
    disease.
4. A young man who is on the verge of failing out of college
    and is under a lot of pressure from his parents to
    succeed.

Think about how each character is likely to express himself

or herself. How do you make the voice of each character sound realistic and distinctive? In what ways do the voices of the characters make the passage work or keep it from working? Note how different the four characters sound from one another. Again, you will only be writing one or two paragraphs for each scene.

Third Person

The third person is perhaps the most common point of view in literature. In the third person, characters and events are observed, either by the main character or an omniscient narrator who never reveals his presence; therefore, even the protagonist is referred to by the appropriate third person pronoun ("he" or "she").

The following paragraph is the most important paragraph in this book, so please read it carefully!

Many beginning writers ask, "What is the difference between third person omniscient and third person attached POVs?" The answer lies in one word: distance. In the omniscient POV, there is significant distance, or sense of disconnection, between the third person narrator and the reader. The reader is very much aware that he is being "told" a story by a storyteller who never presents himself, but is nonetheless a presence in the story. The novel is told in the voice of an unseen, all-knowing third person narrator. In the attached POV, the imaginary distance between the narrator and reader is greatly reduced; the writer is trying to create the illusion that the reader is in the story, almost part of the story. The writer is not trying to tell a story so much as trying to show a story. To do this, the writer using the attached POV gets into the mind of his protagonist and shows us what that character is feeling, thinking and observing. The reader is virtually unaware of anything in the novel unless it comes through the perceptions of the protagonist. Therefore the sense of a narrator, or storyteller, is nearly obliterated.

Third Person Attached POV

Since we believe the attached POV is more effective and easier to work with than the omniscient POV, especially for beginning writers, we will discuss it first. This is the POV created and frequently used by American author Henry James. His novella, *A Turn of the Screw*, is a good example of the technique. Ernest Hemingway's *The Old Man in the Sea* and Stephen King's *The Shining* are other, more recent examples.

Just what is a third person attached POV?

As indicated above, third person attached POV focuses on the thoughts, feelings and observations of one character at a time, frequently for the entire length of the novel. (In this regard, the third person attached resembles the first person POV.) This "POV character" is not aware of anything he cannot imagine, hear, observe, guess or otherwise sense. For example, he cannot be aware of the direct thoughts of other people, but he can guess what they are thinking based on their expressions, movements, tone of voice, conversation and so on.

The following passage is in the third person attached POV. In this passage, the reader is aware of both the POV character's thoughts and feelings.

> Hal walked up to the woman, then hesitated. He felt his mouth gape open, and he quickly snapped it closed. He had asked women to dance with him dozens of times before at a dozen different clubs, but this woman was different. She wasn't just pretty, she was a work of art. Her hair was not blonde but yellow gold. Her eyes weren't just blue but bright sky blue, set in a strong but finely-detailed face. When she turned to face him and he realized he was caught in the steady blue beam of her gaze, he felt his resolve slip away from him like water leaking through his cupped hands. How could he…how could any mere male…be worthy

enough to speak to this angel, let alone press his barbaric body next to hers in dance?

The third person attached POV in this paragraph helps the reader understand Hal as a person, not by telling us about Hal's reaction to the beautiful woman, but by showing us his reaction to her, by depicting her in his thoughts. He believes her eyes are "sky blue," her gaze "blue," her aspect that of "an angel." We see his feelings of inadequacy, which he vividly describes in terms of leaking and the incongruity of his and her body. All these feelings and thoughts are rendered in an intimate and personal way. In this regard, the attached POV is very much like the first person POV, only indirect instead of direct. The narrator who is revealing Hal's thoughts is just barely present in the mind of the reader. We understand that Hal is a sensitive, perhaps even a shy man with some doubts about his self-worth.

In contrast, here is the scenic, or distant, third person unattached POV version of this paragraph. Notice how flat and impersonal it sounds compared to the third person attached version. The narrator who tells us what Hal cannot imagine is a stronger presence here.

> To Hal, the woman's hair looked yellow gold and her eyes were the color of the sky. When she turned to face him, it was as if he were trapped by her eyes. He no longer felt like dancing with her, because he did not think he was good enough for her. She was an angel. He could not imagine himself or any other man pressing himself up against her delicate body.

Because of the closeness that third person attached POV brings to the story, we often suggest that beginning writers work in this POV.

POV Exercise Four

Objective: To write a passage in the third person attached POV

Part 1

Imagine that Hal in the preceding sample passage has been persuaded into asking another woman to dance—but this woman is unfortunately quite plain. What are his thoughts, feelings and reactions to this woman and his predicament? Before, he felt himself unworthy; how does he feel about himself now?

Using the third person attached POV, write a paragraph in which Hal sizes up the homely woman. Remember, all observations, thoughts and feelings must be Hal's.

Part 2

Write your own third person attached passage. It does not need to be any longer than 2 pages. We've listed a few sample scenarios below, but you are free to make up your own.

1. Mark, who has recently lost his little boy in an accident, is sitting in the park brooding to himself when a young child spontaneously comes up to him and asks him, "What's wrong?" Write the scene in the third person, with POV attached to Mark. How does he feel? Is he angry, moved to tears, unmoved...or does he rejoice in the child's selfless gesture? Or does Mark feel some combination of these reactions?

2. Lady Stella, an 18th century maiden who has just wed the Duke of Burleigh, is lying in her bed in her room on her wedding night, anxiously awaiting her husband. She loves him deeply, but is both fearful and expectant. He staggers into her room drunk and collapses on the floor by her bed. Write the scene in third person in

Stella's POV. How does she feel? What will she do?

3. The dwarven fortress of Quarg is under attack by an
    army of Sleeth, the lizard men from the north. Grumel,
    a young dwarven ensign, has been ordered by his
    commanding officer to lead a squadron on a suicide
    mission. Grumel knows the mission is hopeless and that
    the Sleeth can be defeated by other means. Does he
    confront his officer, accept the mission, or play along
    with the officer's demands, intending to try some tricks
    of his own? Write the scene in third person in Grumel's
    perspective. Show the desperation of his situation. Use
    your imagination!

POV Exercise Five

Objective: To rewrite a scene in first person POV into third person attached POV

Part 1

Remember this passage about Tad the stableboy and Ice Age, the race horse? Read it again.

> I said they couldn't give up on her. Ice Age was too good a horse. Doc wanted to put her down, but I said she deserved another chance, there must be something Doc could do. He shrugged. "She's in pain," he said. "Even if this disease didn't cripple her completely, the pain would be on and off. She'll never run again, that's clear. I say let her go."
>
> Mr. Schmidt, who owned Ice Age, ran his hand over her swollen leg. "Isn't there something you can give her?" he said. "You know…a painkiller? I've got a fortune in this horse. She's supposed to run in the Breeder's Cup next week."
>
> Doc shook his head. I knew what he was thinking: Lame horses dosed with painkillers usually ran themselves into shock until they fell and broke a leg. I patted Ice Age's neck and felt a tear run down my cheek. "You can't do that, Mr. Schmidt," I whispered.
>
> "Hell I can't!" he snapped. "She's my horse, and I say she runs."
>
> "Then get yourself another vet," said Doc, and he turned abruptly and strode out of the stable.

Schmidt and spat into the straw. "Tad, go call Dr. Finster. He'll get this nag up and running," he said.

I stroked the mare's soft muzzle. I didn't want her to think that I had abandoned her. My eyes were so full of tears that everything was a blur, including Schmidt's red, angry face. I was so heartbroken, so enraged, so utterly devastated that nothing seemed to make sense anymore.

"Get yourself another boy," I told him. But I didn't walk from the stable. Once I got out of the stall, far enough away from Ice Age so I wouldn't spook her, I ran.

Part 2

Rewrite this scene in the third person, with POV attached to Tad. What is he feeling? What is he thinking? Remember our earlier discussion about pressure and conflict, those devices which force a character to react. Don't be afraid to expand on the original first-person version. Your first few lines might read something like this:

Tad didn't want to give up on her. Ice Age was too good a horse, a sweet horse, a fast horse. In some way she was his horse.

"It's best for her if I put her down," Doc said softly.

No! Tad reached out and grabbed Doc's forearm. "You can't. She's a great horse, she deserves a chance." Even as he spoke he felt a cold spot of fear begin to grow in his stomach. "Isn't there anything you can do?"

Note that the eight lines above are the equivalent of the first three of the first-person version. That is because the third person often allows more room for detail and expansion.

Do you like this passage better in the first person or the third person attached? Why? Which offers the better picture of Tad's emotional dilemma?

POV Shifting

POV shifting occurs when the writer switches abruptly from the point of view of one character to the point of view of another. In extreme cases we have noted up to seven POVs expressed on two consecutive manuscript pages. Such rampant disregard for POV consistency is called "head-hopping" by some editors. Head-hopping is endemic in sloppy fiction and should be avoided by beginning writers. "Attached" means what it says: POV is stuck like glue to the POV character, until and if there is reason and opportunity to switch.

When is it appropriate to change POV characters in an attached viewpoint? We recommend that the beginning writer using attached POV craft the bulk of a novel in a single viewpoint. If it is necessary to include another POV, such as that of the antagonist or romantic interest or other major character, it is best to begin a new chapter for that specific viewpoint, or at least a new scene. Remember, you should be asking yourself, "Whose story is this?" throughout the novel. The answer to this question is almost always your main POV character.

POV Exercise Six

Objective: To recognize and correct POV shifting

Part 1

Using a pencil, mark an "X" or checkmark directly in the book each time the attached viewpoint shifts to another character in the following passage from a historical romance. Each time a shift occurs, name the character POV shifts to.

Lord Walter strode up to Diana and gripped her wrist. He'd find out from her, he vowed, just what she had been doing in the company of that blackguard, Robin Faulksmouth. "Out with it, woman! What business did you have with this lowlife?"

Diana pulled her arm away. How dare he lay his hand on hers so roughly! "What drives you to enquire, my lord? You have no claim on me, I think. Therefore am I not free to converse with whomever I please?"

Diana's maid, Rebecca, shivered at her mistress's sharp tone of voice. The angry faces of the lord and lady frightened her. Stepping back, she begged to be excused.

"Begone then," intoned Diana, waving the girl away with one hand. "I myself am about to quit this dreadful place." The sooner she left Lord Walter's estate the better, she told herself. If his lordship probed too deeply, he would find out the troubling truth surrounding herself and Robin.

"Mistress, you are not leaving now, nor are you leaving at all until you explain yourself."

Grasping her by the shoulders, Lord Walter guided Diana to a chair and forced her to sit down. He had never seen a more obstinate woman before in his entire life. He'd need a glass of brandy if he were to deal with her further. "Harry!" he called to his manservant.

Harry, who had been standing outside the door, entered the drawing room. He was amazed to see his master bending down over a seated lady who glared up at him with fire and hatred in her amber eyes. Barely recovering his composure, Harry stepped forward. "Yes, sir?"

"The decanter. Quickly." With a tip of his head Lord Walter indicated the black liquor cabinet behind him. Harry could be so slow at times.

"This is scarcely the time for refreshment," growled Diana. She glanced at the manservant, trying to decide if he would come to her aid or not. "Lord Walter, pray release your grip. You're hurting me."

Yes, POV shifts with every single paragraph. This creates a very fractured effect as the reader tries to project herself in several characters' minds at once. An extreme example of head-hopping, this passage makes for a very confusing point of view and a generally unreadable piece.

Part 2

Rewrite the preceding scene in either Lord Walter's or Diana's POV using a third person attached viewpoint. Afterward, note how much easier your rewrite is to read. That is because you no longer have to mentally "shift gears" from one character's thoughts to another's as you are reading.

Drawbacks to the Third Person Attached POV

The third person attached POV is not without other drawbacks. No less a writer than John Gardner decried the attached POV, claiming it encouraged ridiculous introspection and self-absorption on the part of the POV character. (For his spoof on the attached POV, read his book, *The Art of the Novel*). Gardner does make a good point; it is possible to write badly in any POV, and third person attached, like first person, does leave itself open to inner monologues and over-emoting. Nevertheless, we find that third person attached POV is the most effective POV for the beginning writer.

Omniscient POV, or Omniscient Narration

The third person omniscient narration is the Grand Old Man of literary viewpoints. In the 18th and 19th centuries, when the novel was indeed "novel" or new, most long fiction was written in the omniscient POV, narrated by a Godlike voice able to understand and reveal every character's thoughts, interpret all actions, presage all events and in general control and shape the entire story. Gabriel Garcia Marquez's *One Hundred Years of Solitude*, Austen's *Pride and Prejudice*, the short stories of Karen Blixen and most of the fiction of Victor Hugo, Sir Walter Scott, Charles Dickens, E.M. Forster, Thomas Hardy, Nathaniel Hawthorne and Leo Tolstoy are all written in the omniscient POV. The omniscient narration is far less popular today, though it is still a valid POV alternative for many writers.

Crafting an omniscient POV depends on creating an omniscient narrator. The omniscient narrator's voice is all-pervasive, and he is as much a presence in the story as any other character. Spewing out a story, slipping in and out of characters' viewpoints, making comparisons and expressing personal opinions willy-nilly does not create an omniscient novel. Creating a consistent, omniscient voice does.

The earliest and most basic examples of the omniscient POV are folk tales, fables and fairy tales, which exist in virtually every culture. The emphasis in these stories is either on a plot or a moral as opposed to character development. An omniscient narrator is absolutely necessary to the fairy tale in several ways: 1) to tie together various parts of often complex story lines; 2) to ride herd on an often large cast of characters; 3) to introduce the element of magic or the supernatural, which many of these stories rely on; and 4) to handle the scope of the story, which may involve ancient times, royal families, battles, farflung kingdoms, monsters and other disparate, "large" subjects. This is how the narrator can get away with saying such things as "Once upon a time" and "They lived happily ever after."

Some novels are better suited for the omniscient POV than others. In some cases, the omniscient POV can give a sense of containment to long, involved, rambling novels. Complex science fiction and fantasy novels or talelike stories, such as the *Lord of the Rings* trilogy by J.R. Tolkien, need the voice of an all-seeing narrator to guide the reader through an intricate landscape populated by diverse creatures. So do family sagas and historical novels of tremendous breadth and scope, such as Leo Tolstoy's novel, *Anna Karenina*. Most modern literary novels and genre novels—including romance, horror, western and mystery novels—are rarely rendered in omniscient narration. They are primarily focused on character development, whereas the omniscient narration emphasizes setting, plot and theme.

Here is an example of omniscient narration, the opening of Leo Tolstoy's *Anna Karenina*.

All happy families are like one another; each unhappy family is unhappy in its own way.

Everything was in confusion in the Oblonsky household. The wife had found out that the husband had had an affair with their French governess and had told him that she could not go on living in the same house with him. This situation had now gone on for three days and was felt acutely by the husband and wife themselves, by all the members of the family, and by their servants. All the members of the family and the servants felt that there was no sense in their living together under the same roof and that people who happened to meet at any country inn had more in common with one another than they, the members of the Oblonsky family and their servants. The wife did not leave her own rooms, and the husband had not been home for three days. The children ran about all over the house looking lost; the English governess had quarreled with the housekeeper and had written to a friend to ask her to find her a new place; the chef had left the house the day before, at dinnertime; the under-cook and the driver had given notice.

Who is telling the story? It isn't in the husband's POV, nor in the wife's, nor a member of the family or servant's POV. It is the unseen narrator, the hidden storyteller—the omniscient voice—which is telling us the story. This opening establishes the story as being about a family, an entire household, and so the consequence of one event (the wife's discovery of the husband's affair) causes a chain of reactions that affect not only the principle characters (husband and wife), but also the secondary and tertiary characters (from the children to the servants). The opening, which juggles many characters at once, is very distant, but it also sets the scope of the novel.

While the omniscient POV is the hardest POV to write successfully, for novels of great scope and depth, it is frequently the only one which is appropriate.

POV Exercise Seven

Objective: To write in third person omniscient POV

Part 1

Write—that is, retell—an omniscient tale. It could be a folk tale, fable, fairy tale, tall tale, cautionary tale or ghost story from any culture. You may also choose stories which have a specific author, such as Hans Christian Andersen or Washington Irving, but are written in the tradition of third person omniscient folk narratives. Below are some examples, but you may choose your own from any source.

1. Rapunzel
2. Any story about Paul Bunyan
3. Goldilocks and the Three Bears
4. The Princess and the Pea
5. The Legend of Sleepy Hollow
6. The Monkey's Paw
7. Ali Baba and the Forty Thieves
8. Any of the Anansi stories from Africa
9. Noah and the Flood or any other biblical story
10. The Adventures of Tom Thumb

Note how often repetition is used in folk tales. In "The Tinderbox," for example, the soldier meets three similar dogs at different times, and in "The Glass Mountain," the shepherd boy must try to ride up the mountain on three different occasions on three different horses. Why do you think repetition is so common in these tales? What was the storyteller trying to do?

Part 2

Choosing from the list on page 135 or from another source, rewrite an omniscient folk story or fairy tale, putting an original spin on it. For example, what if the bears came to visit Goldilocks? What if Ichabod Crane discovered that the Headless Horseman was a ruse? What if Aladdin's lamp fell into the hands of the president of the United States? You get the picture.

Part 3

Write your own folk-style story or fable in the third person omniscient POV, complete with third person narrator. This is not easy to do. Consider relating a personal anecdote in the third person instead of the first person. Perhaps you've been to a crazy, wacky party...or were on a TV quiz show...or had a disastrous honeymoon. Tell us about it through an omniscient narrator.

Remember that many fairy tales and fables have morals, themes or "lessons"; they are instructive or illustrative. The parable of the good Samaritan, for instance, was meant to illustrate the virtue of brotherly love. Consider writing that sort of story.

Distance and the Omniscient Narrator

The third person omniscient POV offers more distance between reader and material than any other literary POV except scenic/cinematic (which offers too much distance). More distance means that the reader is less intimately involved with the thinking processes of the main character. The added feeling of distance in the omniscient POV is both the beauty and undoing of this point of view. On the plus side, this POV frequently reveals the thoughts of many characters, even minor ones. Therefore, we have immediate access to important plot information, and can go into any character's thoughts in order to retrieve this information. There is much less tendency to become bogged down in inner monologues, since we are not really "inside" any one character's mind for long periods of time. In fact, we are often outside characters' viewpoints and inside the mind of the omniscient narrator.

A word of caution to the beginning writer: The omniscient POV is not something to undertake lightly. Because it is so broad in scope, it is difficult to pull off effectively and, of course, it depends on the writer's ability to craft a compelling narrative voice. Also, as we've discussed, the omniscient POV is not best suited to most novels.

When handled poorly or inappropriately, without regard to the necessity of creating the "character" of the narrator, POV sometimes becomes too distant and results in the scenic or cinematic POV.

Scenic POV

In the scenic POV, characters' thoughts and actions are very distant from the reader. We do not "get into the character's mind" on any level, but are merely told what is happening in the story, as if a reporter were on the scene, taking notes. Because of its vast distance and lack of emotion, the scenic POV is rarely used successfully in long fiction. However, this POV can occasionally be very effective in short stories and some nonfiction, especially when a great deal of distance is required by the writer. For example, in *In Cold Blood* by Truman Capote (a work of nonfiction) a brutal, cold-hearted murder is described in the scenic POV. The added distance contrasts with and therefore emphasizes the detachment of the murderers, the outrageousness of their crime and the inhuman, uncaring nature of their conduct.

In general, beginning writers do not write in the scenic POV as a matter of strategy. Sometimes their scenic writing is the result of an aborted attempt to write in the omniscient POV, or even the attached POV, but most often a writer is simply unaware that POV exists. When told that they have not attached POV to their characters, these writers will counter, "But I am attached to the main character. Every scene is about her." It is all too possible, of course, to write a scene "about" a character that is not in her POV...or anyone else's.

Here is a typical scenic paragraph of very flat, distanced writing, with virtually no tone and frequently no voice. You can almost see the "reporter" on the site, taking notes, recording actions and words but little else.

> Todd and his friend Willie walked into The Sweet Life and began looking at all the candy displays. Todd wanted to buy gummy worms in a container of crushed chocolate cookies, but he didn't have enough money. He stared at the gumballs for a while, but finally decided on buying a small package of Boston baked beans,

which were really peanuts in candy shells, and a Nuclear Holocaust jawbreaker. He'd never had either candy before, and they looked pretty good.

Willie had only fifty cents, so he had to settle for a box of chocolate-coated raisins and a miniature Mounds bar. As they took their purchases to the cashier and counted out their dimes and nickels, she offered them little sample candies in the shape of animals, which Todd took but Willie declined. "That's for kids," said Willie, who was all of ten.

Well, there certainly is a lot going on here, but we might as well be reading about it in a newspaper. Candy is perhaps one of the most emotionally-charged items in a child's life, yet this passage has no inkling of passion or even faint stirrings of feelings. Is this a routine purchase for the boys, or is it special? We certainly can't tell from the POV. Because the writing is devoid of emotion, the scene is flat and serves no purpose except to fill up space and take up the characters' time. Notice also that the passage is not really in anyone's POV, neither that of a character nor a strong narrator.

POV Exercise Eight

Objective: To rewrite a scenic POV passage using third person attached POV

Read the following flat, scenic, authorial scene. Note that it is currently written in what we refer to as the "they" POV. It is as if the author is treating two characters as one, as if they both think, act and feel the same. This is to be avoided. Notice also that this paragraph works too hard to tell us what both men are thinking. How might you reveal their thoughts and feelings without blatantly narrating them?

> When the waitress returned with their beers, Kevin and Rod placed their orders. After she left, the two close friends chatted a little while, talking about work at the insurance company and reminiscing over the adventures they'd had growing up together in the little Iowa farming community of River Springs. They had both also seen many dangers while serving together in Viet Nam, and their voices grew quiet as they recounted some near misses and remembered the friends who never returned. In fact, both men missed the active life and yearned for a way to bring the excitement and thrills of their former life into their boring present one.

Rewrite this scene in no more than two pages using either the third person attached POV (choose Kevin or Rod). Think of what you want this scene to say about either Kevin, Rod or both men.

Some things to keep in mind:

1. This piece will be easier to rewrite and more effective in the third person attached POV, in which you can concentrate on revealing the personality of a single character.

2. Think about why Kevin and Rod have gotten together that night. Have they not seen each other in a long time, or do they have a mutual problem they must resolve?

3. What sort of people are Kevin and Rod? How are they the same? How are they different?

4. How important are the men's earlier reminiscences? What seems to be the point of this passage? Where might the writer be taking this story?

5. What would change about this passage if Kevin and Rod had met only a few days earlier? Would you still be able to write a story about men who yearned for excitement in their lives? What difference does it make that they are old friends?

Your passage need not answer all these questions and probably won't. They are just kindling for the mind, a way to help you think about the possibilities for drama or meaning inherent in this flat passage.

The Cinematic POV

One of the most important tasks of the fiction writer is to create three-dimensional characters who react to events in the plot, changing and developing as the plot unfolds. By exploring the character's thoughts, feelings and reactions to events, the writer allows the character to experience deeper and deeper insights into his behavior and that of others.

This ___ does not take place in the cinematic POV, which is really _____ ___ form of the scenic POV. The cinematic POV is as close as one can get to an absence of point of view and is virtually devoid of interpretation or feeling. In the cinematic POV, narrative proceeds as if the reader is observing actors, props and actions on a movie set through the lens of a camera. In a movie, feelings and thoughts can be expressed through dialogue, or the expressions of actors and other visuals, but that is not the case in a novel. Characters' hopes, dreams, fears, emotions and thoughts must all be expressed or implied through words.

In the cinematic POV, characters are reduced to cardboard figures acting out the action in the plot in front of a passionless, almost mechanical narrator (the camera). That is why, when we get a letter at the agency describing a manuscript as "a great plot for a movie," we cringe and shudder. We just know that the writer is envisioning a plot-driven, two-dimensional story with paper-thin characters that he can manipulate at will.

The hallmarks of the cinematic POV are camera techniques adapted to the page. Note that no character observes the details in the samples below; they are seen by an invisible camera.

1. *Zooms*—The writer might "zoom in" on a character's face: "The lines on her face tightened as her lips inched upward into a smile." Describe details only when they

are important to plot, character or setting.

2. *Pull backs*—Here the POV seems to "draw back" from a scene to reveal or imply a foreground and a background: "The woman stood by a pool, surrounded by shrubs and flowers, with pines in the background. The San Gabriel Mountains loomed in the distance." Make sure to establish setting, either in an omniscient or attached POV.

3. *Pans*—The cinematic POV might pan a scene as a camera would: "The farmhouse sat next to a duck pond; a girl, emerging from a nearby stand of oak trees, approached the pond." The writer should simply establish the setting and let the POV character observe the scene.

4. *Cues*—Here, the "camera" pulls very far back, almost to the point that we can imagine we hear the director shouting instructions to the actors and crew: "A burst of laughter comes from Chet's and Regina's table." The laughter has to come from the characters.

5. *Props*—Inconsequential lists of unimportant physical objects or details give the impression of the presence of props: "The house had a roomy kitchen which was full of shelves. On the shelves were cans of soup, tomato paste and creamed corn, as well as bottles of salad dressing, bags of potato chips and jars of instant coffee." Lists of items are important details, but only when they are meaningful items.

6. *Stage directions*—These are lists of inconsequential actions that a character indulges in to no purpose. They sound like the directions to actors in a stageplay or screenplay—"Dave opens the refrigerator, looks around, shuffles a few containers about and finally chooses a can

of beer. Then he closes the door, opens the beer can and takes a gulp of Miller Lite." This line could be rewritten along the lines of, "Dave got a beer from the refrigerator and took a sip." (We'll assume he opened it.)

7. *Present tense*—The present tense can be used legitimately in fiction, usually short stories, to create a sense of urgency and immediacy. However, the present tense is often coupled with the cinematic POV to recreate the feel of the distance afforded by the eye of the camera, as if the actions in the novel are being recorded mechanically, on the spot. Notice how much stronger "Napoleon loved Josephine" sounds than "Napoleon loves Josephine." The latter sounds like graffiti.

8. *Cuts*—Writers using the cinematic POV often "cut" to a scene without any transition, or bridge, from scene to scene; this is fine in the movies, where visuals provide a continuum, but not in a novel.

None of these techniques help advance character or plot; indeed, they seem to do little more than provide props, camera angles and backdrops for a screenplay, and a novel is not a screenplay. While the movie or screenplay relies on visual images, the novel relies on words to imply images and actions and thus help the reader create her own visuals.

POV Exercise Nine

Objective: To recognize and rewrite cinematic writing

Read the paragraph below.

> In the foreground is a rustic shack about twenty feet long and fifteen feet across. On the roof of the structure is a collection of stones, some scattered over the cedar shingles, some clustered in groups on the corners of the roof. Some of the stones are full of fossils, indicating that they have come from the riverbed of Roaring River, only a quarter mile away. Along the side of the shack is a rough-hewn pine bench about three feet long. It awaits the owner of the hut, who has always in the past taken in the bench during bad weather. In the background is a glittering ridge, already wearing the white tokens of the winter storms soon to come.

Part 1

Jot down the ways in which this sample shows itself to be in the cinematic POV. It is, for example, in the present tense (not always a dead giveaway). What other "techniques" suggest that this piece was written with producers, not publishers, in mind?

Part 2

Rewrite the paragraph in either first person or third person attached POV in order to correct the distant, artificial sound of the cinematic POV.

Authorial Intrusion

Authorial intrusion occurs when the writer himself walks into his story and begins expressing his opinions on the plot, characters, or topics of relevance to the story. This kind of writing is a sure sign that a novel's point of view is in trouble. It is almost always an error and never fails to stick out from the rest of the writing like a bandaged head wound.

Authorial intrusion is usually the hallmark of the scenic or cinematic POV, and it's easy to understand why. If a novel uses an extremely distant POV, we can imagine that a writer might feel obliged to give the impression that a point of view does indeed exist. Therefore, he gives us his own POV. This technique, unfortunately, doesn't work.

No third person viewpoint, including attached and omniscient, is immune from authorial intrusion, although first person narratives are usually free of it.

Authorial intrusion occurs when the writer breaks out of what John Gardner called the "fictional dream," that is, the illusion of an alternate reality that most fiction writers strive so hard to create. By directly addressing readers with his own thoughts or bits of wisdom and instruction, the writer in essence tells his readers, "This story isn't really happening. I'm just making it up, and I can do whatever I want with it. I am basically manipulating your thoughts, and now you are aware of that fact."

A writer is intruding in his novel whenever he:

1. *Gives his personal view on a topic*: "George found out that Drake had AIDS, which is primarily a lifestyles disease."

2. *Gives away information in a blatant, obvious fashion, revealing what characters do not know*: "Little did Parker realize that Louise was really having an affair with

Michael," or "Parker didn't see Louise at the restaurant, or he would have realized immediately that she was dating Michael."

3. *Stands up on a literary soapbox and begins writing an opinion essay in the middle of a novel*: "With tears in her eyes, the girl admitted she had been abused by her father when she was five. Child abuse is a terrible crime and should be punished harshly. The laws in this country regarding child abuse are much too mild and are not enforced consistently." (It is surprising how many very fine writers succumb to this writing problem!)

4. *Uses the omniscient voice but tells the reader information that is obviously coming from the author, not the omniscient narrator*: "Buck decided to stay the night in Jacksonville. Jacksonville is a miserable town with few decent accommodations. The food is bad and the people are surly and prejudiced."

5. *Stops the story to "fill the reader in on" a specific nugget of information, such as the main character's childhood or the laws regarding euthanasia in the state of Florida*. This interruption is akin to a commercial break, or a newsflash, and has no place at all in a novel. Information which is important to the reader's understanding of the plot, setting or characters must be woven naturally into the story, not supplied as an afterthought by the writer.

In conventional novels, there is never a need for authorial intrusion. While the writer might feel he is imparting valuable information to the reader, he is instead only stopping the story, distracting the reader from the character's situation and in general calling attention to the fact that writing is an artifice.

Of course a writer can express his opinions; that is one of the purposes of characters. A writer can create a character who expresses the writer's viewpoint, or any other, for that matter. Thus, if you wish to write about the injustice of racism, show us a character being discriminated against, or a character rousing others to take action against racial injustice. This will be ever so much stronger and more effective than stepping into the story and telling the reader your opinions on the subject.

Unless you are writing an omniscient narrative and are certain that you are using it correctly, avoid omniscient remarks such as, "If Bernard had gone to Toledo, he could have avoided the accident." It is distracting and distancing, and the reader will wonder who is imparting this information. In most cases, most information can be relayed through the POV character or through dialogue.

POV Exercise Ten

Objective: To recognize and correct authorial intrusion

Part 1

The following passage is written almost entirely in scenic POV with heavy authorial intrusion, with a brief interlude in one character's POV. Read the passage and jot down some notes on the ways the writer uses authorial intrusion to try—unsuccessfully—to advance the story. He actually ends up stopping the story in several places. Where does the writer:

a)   try to "explain" what is happening?
b)   supply background information?
c)   tease the reader with his (the writer's) understanding of the story? and
d)   espouse his own ideas and opinions?

Note that the writer is trying so hard to disseminate information in his own viewpoint in the first two paragraphs that he changes his topic with virtually every sentence, entirely losing the thread of the plot, which started at the airforce base. Why do you think the writer addresses the reader outright near the end, referring to "you?"

It was a boring evening at the Marldale Airforce Base, forty air miles southwest of Johnsville and ten miles southwest of Phoenix International Airport. The compound was on round-the-clock alert, its special forces unit (SFU) team ready to go into action. The team was formed to provide immediate response against a threat until support, such as the local police and FBI, could arrive. The team members are recruited from elite forces of the U.S. mili-

tary, including the Navy Seals. Their chief task
is to conduct covert operations in civilian areas,
and they do an excellent job of this. Many lives
have been saved because of their quick action.

The SFU team had been assigned to cover
certain critical staff members at the Desert Institute Lab, where personnel were working on the
Greenfield Project. Lewis National Laboratory,
twenty miles away from DIL, was also working
on the project. Lewis was one of the largest and
most important labs of its kind in the entire
country, employing over a thousand workers. It
was instrumental to Allied success during World
War II, and The University of Arizona still
operates the lab for the U.S. Department of
Defense.

The telephone rang once, and Sergeant
Wallace of the SFU team picked it up and said
hello. He hoped it wasn't a routine communications check. He wished it was an assignment of
some sort. It is very tedious to be on alert at an
airforce base, because most of the time you just
hang around waiting for something to do. You
can't go out anywhere or call anyone. You just
have to try to pass the time as best you can and
wish for someone to call you. That is why most
people who have this sort of position either hate
it or are very laid back.

Wallace was not an easy-going guy, and he
was about to get his wish for some action.

Part 2

This passage is badly written, mainly because of the writer's overindulgence in authorial intrusion. Perhaps if the POV were attached to Wallace or a strong narrative voice it would be easier to tell the story and avoid the tendency to explain every detail.

Try rewriting the passage in the attached or omniscient POV. Unless background information is essential to the reader's understanding, don't give it out. Create Wallace's boring world as he waits for "something to happen." What will Wallace feel when that telephone rings with news of a break-in at the Desert Institute Lab? What sort of person is Wallace? Show us that person. These are the details your reader is interested in, but they must not come in the author's voice.

Putting It All Together

Now you are ready to put to use all that you have learned about point of view in this important section. Remember, without an effective POV, even the most imaginative and fast-paced fiction will fall flat on its typeface. That is because a writer must create the impression that the action of the novel is truly happening to people who are truly alive; thus someone must be observing and reacting to the characters and events in the novel.

All the exercises on the following pages pertain to a variety of viewpoints. If you need help to clarify which is which, go back and review the sections discussing the individual POVs. Do not be disappointed if you have difficulty identifying or writing each sample; these exercises are not easy, and some may require more than a little effort. You'll find your effort will be repaid in spades once you've developed a good feel for the effective use of POV.

POV Exercise Eleven

Objective: To recognize POV in published novels

Read the beginning passages of several of your favorite novels and identify the POV of each. Which type seems to be the most common? Are any of these novels written in a scenic or cinematic POV?

POV Exercise Twelve

Objective: To identify POV

Read the short excerpts below and identify them by POV: First person (FP), third person attached (TPA), third person omniscient (TPO), scenic (S), cinematic (C). Indicate authorial intrusion (AI) whenever appropriate.

1. This Shane Cameron was a big man, the tallest in the crowded room, and his boots reached well below the knees of his long, lean legs.
2. Janice walked into the garden and began talking to Phil, who turned away after a few minutes and loped off into the woods.
3. "I don't believe a single word you've told me," he said, spraying saliva in my face as he spoke, "and neither will Father."
4. It was a beautiful dog, that Afghan hound, slender and nervous; its silky coat shook like a tambourine as it walked.
5. During the days he spent in bed, feeling slowly returned to Gordon's benumbed hands and feet. People who have suffered hypothermia frequently take a long time to recover full feeling in their extremities.
6. The queen ran her hand over the jeweled hilt of the dagger: should she use it against Wolfstein, she thought— or herself?
7. Cornelia stood slightly to the left of the huge fir tree, which was about five paces behind her and seven paces from the rose bed in front of her.
8. The cool wind reminded Frank of the autumn day he had first kissed Julia.

9. Sidewinder was a rollicking town, brand new and raring to go, as if it had sprung up fully formed from the yellow Texas dirt one morning after a desert rainfall.

10. Every evening without fail during my childhood, Mother would sing to us children. It was not the songs themselves that were important, but the fact that she sung them to us.

11. Rafferty buys a Zagnut bar, peels off the wrapper, throws it in a nearby trash can, and sinks his teeth into the candy.

12. The car drove slowly down the dark street, weaving in and out of shadows and eventually emerging in an empty parking lot.

13. As he made his way home, Craig wondered about Rochelle: It wasn't like her to be the least bit concerned about the welfare of a child.

14. Marsha called Lance and told him she never wanted to see him again. She would later have reason to regret this decision.

POV Exercise Thirteen

Objective: To rewrite a scene in each of the three major POVs

This exercise may prove to be a lot of work, but we think you will find it quite worthwhile.

The following passage is written in the scenic POV, that is, very flat and distanced, without access to any character's thoughts, feelings or mental reactions. It is also full of authorial intrusion. Your mission: Rewrite this passage three times, each in a different POV: once in the first person, once in the third person attached, and once in the omniscient POV. (You may decide to make either the guard or the intruder the protagonist. You may want to assign a name to the main character you choose.) Note the way this passage changes in scope, depth and intensity once you create a viable POV and begin to flesh out the characters. Which version do you like best? Why?

> On Sunday, shortly after three in the morning, the chief of security at the Minneapolis Robotic Research Center was making his rounds through Digby Hall, a complex of buildings near the university campus. As he rounded a corner and checked the first office door to make sure it was locked, he observed a woman coming out of one of the restricted laboratories. The chief walked up to the short, attractive woman, who appeared to be trying to lock the door behind her.
>
> "Ma'am, do you have clearance?" the chief asked softly.
>
> The stranger, who still faced the door, said nothing but continued to jiggle her key in the

lock in an attempt to secure the door. The chief began to suspect something was wrong.

Suddenly the stranger turned and faced the security guard. She pointed her right hand at the chief's face, and he saw that she was holding a gun. The chief began to back up and, at the same time, raised his left arm to his chest, as though to shield himself. He tried to pull his revolver from his holster, but it was too late. He never got the chance.

He didn't see the bright flash of light or hear the roar of the shot, nor did he see the second flash or hear the second roar. He knew he had been shot when he felt the impact of the first bullet. He felt a second impact as the second bullet hit him in the shoulder, sending him sprawling on his back. He was seriously wounded.

Cool Down

Point of view is the single most important topic in this book. That is because so many beginning writers already understand the importance of character and plot development, while so few comprehend what POV is, how it works and why their novels need a consistent, effective point of view.

Once you've understood these POV basics, you should notice a great improvement in your writing. It should be easier to develop characters, explore their thoughts and feelings, and get your readers involved in both the plot and the characters.

If you have read this chapter and completed the exercises and still don't have a good grasp on point of view and how to establish it, you may wish to read our book, *Getting Your Manuscript Sold*, for further information.

8

"Just Do It": Scene and Narrative

Thought is the blossom; language the bud; action the fruit behind it.

—Ralph Waldo Emerson

By now you should have a good idea what a plot is and how it normally progresses throughout a novel. But how is an effective, fast-paced, well-structured, easily understandable and intriguing plot achieved? In this chapter we'll investigate those mysteries, which include the differences between scene and narration, why the successful writer often chooses to "show" a

159

story rather than "tell" it, and how he accomplishes this feat. We'll also discuss the use of suspense, pace, and transitions to make the most out of scenes and the plot in general.

Scene Versus Narrative

A question often asked by the beginning novelist is, what is the difference between a scene and narrative? A scene is a discreet incident in a story, an incident which the writer renders vividly, specifically and for a particular purpose. In a scene, the writer shows the reader what is happening in the story. In narrative, the writer tells the reader what is happening.

For example, if you wished to let the reader know that Agatha is nervous about going out with Jerry, you could simply write, "Agatha was nervous about her date with Jerry." That would be a narrative statement, since the narrator of the story is telling the reader how Agatha felt. On the other hand, you could write a short scene in which you revealed Agatha's nervousness about the date, a scene in which her hands are shaking so badly she can hardly put on makeup; she starts when she sees his photograph; she puts her dress on backward; she voices some of her fears to her mother. By creating this scene, you would show the reader Agatha's nervousness and would not need to mention it outright. The reader himself will be able to visualize Agatha's state of mind and he will have a clearer picture of her personality.

You have no doubt heard the advice, "Show, don't tell," but few new novelists understand what that means. Simply put, it is often advisable and more powerful to create a scene instead of relying on narrative to make a story move forward. Scenes are especially important for revealing crucial meetings, conflicts, conversations, and so on.

For example, instead of telling us, "Jeanne had a crush on her high school Spanish teacher, but he was really trying to seduce her," show us Jeanne and her teacher in a scene, perhaps one in which he is giving her a private tutoring session. If it is in her point of view, show her trying to earn his attention, perhaps telling lies about her accomplishments, or being glad that she wore her favorite dress. Let us "see" her thinking about him, imagining his thoughts. If he says something risqué, Jeanne might misinterpret it or choose to ignore it. If the scene is in his point of view, we will need to be privy to his lustful thoughts and predatory strategies, or even his great neediness. Perhaps he is aware of her innocence, and this adds fuel to his fire...or perhaps he thinks her naiveté is ingenuous and that she is just being coy.

By creating a specific scene, usually complete with dialogue and the thoughts of the protagonist, the writer avoids the pitfall of simply throwing information at the reader and creating a distant, scenic point of view. A scene allows the reader to use his own creativity to understand how the characters feel and to envision what they are going through.

Scene and Narrative Exercise One

Objective: To craft narrative into scenes

The paragraph below, written in narrative form, is from a historical novel set in 11th century Norway. Craft it into a scene between Bent, Ingrid and Olaf. Decide before you write if you wish to use a first person POV or a third person POV attached to any of the three characters. (It is currently in a rather scenic POV.) Assume that this passage takes place at the beginning of a chapter. Don't be afraid to try to use dialogue, even though we have not discussed it yet. Also, you may find that your scene is considerably longer than a paragraph. This is no cause for alarm; narrative tends to compress action, while a scene tends to draw it out and give depth and detail.

It was a dark day in midwinter, and the winds were howling fiercely from the north. In a little anteroom of the great lodge, Bent, the chief of the little community of Norsemen, listened to Olaf. Olaf, a mere farmer, voiced his desire to marry Ingrid, Bent's youngest daughter. When Olaf had finished, Bent pounded his fist once on the table before him, then reconsidered. Bent watched Ingrid carefully, trying to decide what she truly felt for Olaf. She held the farmer's hand so tight her knuckles grew pale, though her face was beet red. Bent was afraid that Ingrid might indeed be in love, or worse yet, with child. He calmed himself a moment and told Olaf and Ingrid to go into the great room where the rest of the family waited, while he thought about Olaf's proposal.

Narrative

If scenes are so important, then when should a writer use narrative? Because writing a novel is, on a basic level, "telling a story," narrative is a valuable tool of the fiction writer. Scenes tend to center on critical actions or events in the story, but there is much material that is better represented through narration. Novelists use narrative to establish the setting of a scene, to indicate the passing of time and the seasons, to craft transitions between scenes and to reveal the thoughts, fears, hopes, dreams and memories of characters. Also, most action scenes are written in narrative form, with very little dialogue and an emphasis on specific physical movements. Such scenes are sometimes called "narrative scenes." In these scenes, the writer "tells" us what happens, usually in the POV of the central character.

For example, here is a "narrative scene" from a historical piece about the Battle of Waterloo. Note that, while the scene is in the POV of Marly, a young dragoon, the emphasis is on the action; no dialogue is necessary, and the result is a smooth flow of active narrative.

> He heard only one note of the bugle call to charge. While he didn't react to it, his horse did, and leaped forward, nearly trampling the animal in front of her. Marly clung to her mane and managed to draw his saber, but he was so close to his fellows that he could do nothing but hold it impotently over his head and force the fierce sounds of his terror from his throat. For a moment he thought of his mother, and then Alice and their little house in Finchely. Fear rose in him like a fever, and he shrieked all the louder to drive it away.

The mass of cavalry engulfing him careened through a thick cloud of black smoke. Marly snapped his eyes and mouth shut, and when he opened them again he saw the French lines directly in front of him, scattering in confusion. A blast ripped at his ears. A horse to his left fell to the ground, screaming, its rider's head a scarlet pulp of flesh and bone. Marly fought the image from his mind and forced himself to stare at the glinting blue uniforms of the French as they turned at bay before the onslaught of thundering English horse.

Narrative also allows the writer to plumb the depths of a character's mind. Imagine that Bea, a schoolgirl, is worried about her father's illness while she is taking a test at school. The writer could write this sort of narrative: "As she began to read the first question, Bea thought about her father and began to feel scared. She laid down her pencil and sat in complete silence, her hands in her lap, staring at the blank paper." Such narrative is flat and straightforward, relying on the character's physical responses alone to deliver meaning. The narrator is clearly present and stronger than the character. POV is not really attached to Bea, since we are not aware of her specific thoughts.

Here is the same passage, rewritten in a stronger, more attached narrative form in a sort of narrative scene:

Bea began to read the first question, something about Spanish explorers in South America, but a little spot of fear began growing in her stomach and she couldn't ignore it. It spread upward into her arms until it stung her fingers and forced her to put down her pencil. She stared at the white surface of the test paper and thought of her father's face—the weary, ashen face she had seen that morning at the breakfast table. Already the disease was beginning to pull him down, conquer him, reduce him to a xeroxed copy of himself. And what could she do to help? Bea thought. There was nothing, nothing at all. She might as well try throwing sticks at a suit of armor.

The thought that her father might die filled her with terror. She couldn't move, she couldn't breathe. A terrible emptiness burned within her and melted tears from her eyes. She tried to make herself grow numb but it was too late.

In general, narrative is an effective tool for advancing both plot and character in a novel. Writers run into trouble if they rely too heavily on narrative to tell the story instead of showing it in carefully selected scenes, complete with dialogue. Of course, the reverse can be true as well: Skipping from scene to scene creates an episodic feel which hampers the flow of the novel. Writing an outline will help you determine which events are so vital that they should be presented in a dramatic manner in scene, and which should be narrated.

Scene and Narrative Exercise Two

Objective: To write a short narrative scene

Imagine that Bent has decided to test Olaf's courage by taking him boar hunting, a dangerous sport. Bent's plans go awry when he is attacked by a bear. Write a short narrative scene in Olaf's POV, no more than 3 pages long, in which the bear attacks Bent and Olaf rescues his prospective father-in-law. Note: Olaf doesn't have to kill the bear; what clever idea might he come up with to save Bent?

The Love Scene

In a love scene, two main characters experience an intimate, personal episode. They might make love...or they might simply sit together in front of a fire, recalling impressions of their wedding day. The scene in which the two protagonists part in *The Remains of the Day* is a sort of love scene, although the characters do not even kiss. They experience intense, intimate feelings toward each other, feelings which ultimately drive them part.

In most modern novels, a love scene does often involve sexual activity between people in love. Even so, a love scene is not a sex scene. The primary purpose of the love scene is to show the reader the depth of the characters' feelings for each other. In other words, the emphasis is on their love, not their love-making. Even if the love scene includes graphic descriptions of the sex act, the reader will be left with an impression of how the characters feel about each other, not the size of their body parts or the variety of positions they use.

A love scene, like any other necessary part of a novel, is used to advance plot or develop characters, possibly both. Its purpose is not simply to titillate the reader, but to reveal the characters' most loving, most intimate feelings. If you don't need to do this, then you don't need a love scene. (Not all those who have sex are in love, of course; see the following section on the sex scene.)

How Does One Write a Love Scene?

First of all, as with any scene, consider point of view. Is the man or woman the POV character? In romance novels, the female protagonist is usually the POV character; however, POV sometimes shifts back and forth from the woman to the man in a love scene. (Note: This is one of the few instances where POV shifting may be acceptable.) Using an attached third person POV will allow you to "get inside the head" of your character(s) and let your readers in on her most personal thoughts and emotions.

Second, consider the meaning of passion. How do people feel when they are in love and sexually aroused? Does the sex act become an expression of their love? How do the characters feel about each other? Try to incorporate those feelings into sexual expression. For example, has the woman suffered a rape when she was younger? Is she somewhat fearful of sex? Is the man aware of this and therefore especially tender and considerate of her during their sexual play?

Try to avoid "lust clichés" such as heaving breasts, skin as soft as a rose petal, or fires in the loins or belly. Also avoid euphemisms such as "manroot" or "love-mound," as well as pornographic terms which could detract from the feelings you are trying to portray. Practical, straightforward terms for body parts, when necessary, are often the most effective, although the language should not sound clinical.

Here is an example of a love scene involving a middle-aged couple. As you read, ask yourself what makes this a love scene. What purpose might it have in a novel?

> Sarah felt a tingling in her stomach as John scooped her into his strong arms. He smelled comfortingly of musk and mint toothpaste. "You're such a little thing," he said, laying her on the bed. The satin sheets were cool under her half-naked body and she shivered. It was not just from the cold, she knew.
>
> "Chilly?" he asked, covering her with a white flannel blanket.

"A little," she answered. She reached for him and pulled him toward her. "I've missed you."

"Me, too," John whispered. He lifted her head and fanned out her silky black hair on the pillow. "You're beautiful, lady."

Sarah nodded. God, how she had missed him! Any other man might comment on her extra pounds, her flabby stomach, her sagging rear end, but John ignored them. Maybe he didn't even see them. Love must be blind, she thought.

But somehow she was not blind to the many lines around his eyes and mouth, or his receding hairline, or the slight paunch that thickened his waist. He was getting older.

"What are you thinking?" John asked, brushing her hair away from her cheeks.

"Your laugh," she answered, tracing the shape of his smile, which reminded her of a crescent moon. "You always see the good things, you know."

"That's because you love me." John kissed her eyes, her lips, her neck. She trembled as a sudden fire ran through her, shattering the cold. Through the blanket he cupped her breasts in his hands, gently at first. Then with his fingers he applied a slight pressure to her nipples and sucked them through the fabric. Sarah sighed deeply.

"Yes, I do love you," Sarah said, pulling back the covers and stripping off her cotton camisole. She watched John as he stared at her. He reminded her of that young teenage boy, so many years ago, seeing her naked body for the first time.

"We haven't changed much, have we?" Sarah whispered as he lowered himself on top of her.

Love wasn't blind, she thought, only a little nearsighted.

Note that, while the language in the passage above is not explicit, the intent is. These people are going to have sex. What differentiates this scene from a sex scene is the motivations of the characters.

Scene and Narrative Exercise Three

Objective: To craft an effective love scene

Remember Shakespeare's brilliant play, Romeo and Juliet? If it's been a long time since you looked at this masterpiece, scan through the play to refresh yourself with it. You'll see that Shakespeare cut right from the wedding night directly to the couple's first morning as man and wife, completely omitting the obvious. Given his times, Old Will could not even attempt to deliver an intimate love scene...but you can! Assume that Romeo and Juliet are a contemporary young people, a little more worldly and little older than Shakespeare made them. Still, they've hurriedly married and know they must part in the morning, because their parents so strongly disapprove of the marriage that Romeo's life will be in danger. (Don't worry about the details of this peculiar situation.)

Write a love scene between this modern Romeo and Juliet, as if you were going to include it in a novel. Concentrate on their feelings for each other, their great love, their great joy at finally being together, and the bittersweet knowledge that they must soon part. Choose to write in either Juliet's or Romeo's attached POV. Remember—you're not trying to compete with Shakespeare's matchless prose here; you're just flexing your fiction-writing skills a little.

The Sex Scene

What if your characters are neither in love nor even very affectionate with each other, but they intend to have sex? If the scene advances plot or develops your characters, you'll probably want to include that scene.

A word of caution here: Don't write a sex scene for the sake of titillation alone. Many beginning writers get the feeling that they are obligated, perhaps by the literary industry itself, to write at least one scene showing explicit sex, a "steamy" scene that has no purpose in the story except to arouse the sexual feelings of the reader. On the contrary, if you don't need a sex scene, don't write one. Write a sex scene, or any other scene, for two purposes only: to advance the story itself, or to show the reader the personality of your characters, chiefly your main character.

In a sex scene, your characters won't be hampered by their need to express their love for each other. On the other hand, if you are merely portraying their lust, then you must ask yourself why. You must be careful not to make the sex scene sound like a digression or diversion for the reader, something "tacked on" to the plot. No, the sex scene must reveal something about the plot or the characters having sex.

How Does One Write a Sex Scene?

One writes a sex scene much like one writes a love scene, but with one important exception: Love is one feeling that won't be on the agenda. That being the case, it's a good idea to ask yourself, "Why are these people making love?"

It could be for plot purposes. Perhaps the woman wants to make her husband or boyfriend jealous, or maybe the man has bet someone he can seduce so many women in so many days.

Chances are, though, the sex scene is used to develop a character. Is the woman so insecure that she sleeps with any man who can offer her immediate but temporary validation of her womanhood? Is the man on the rebound from a previous romance or marriage and therefore rather hesitant? If so, we need to see these characters' feelings and let them develop.

Here is an example of a sex scene. Notice that the woman has something other than love on her mind.

> Moira took Rob by the hand and led him over a stony field to a grove of pine trees. The needles from the trees were soft and brown under her bare feet. The noise from the picnic grew more and more faint.
>
> "Surely they won't see us here," she murmured, stopping in the grove. A ripple of fear ran across her shoulder blades, and she was surprised by how good it felt. What if her husband did see her and Rob in the heat of sex? What could the old man do to stop them?
>
> The thought made her smile.
>
> Rob tried to encircle her with his arms, but she ducked under his elbow, laughing. Moira watched his eyes widen in surprise, but an instant later he began to grin. "Oh, you're a tease, you are," he muttered. Moira darted into the trees and led Rob on a merry chase, around one stout tree and on to the next, until her foot caught in an exposed root. She flopped to the earth in a cloud of pine needles, trying to stifle her laughter as she fell.
>
> Then Rob was on top of her, clutching at her

breasts and forcing his mouth against hers. She wanted to give in to his rough passion, to feel a real man pressing against her, moving inside her, but she wanted the moment to last. Moira wrenched herself free of his kiss, cupped his chin in one hand and forced his head back until he was obliged to put a stop to his brainless pawing.

"Haven't you ever heard of slow and easy?" she asked. He stared at her dumbfounded, like a deer caught in the glare of headlights. She sat up, cocked her head and laughed at him, twirling a lock of her red-gold hair around one finger.

Rob rose to his knees and brushed a shower of pine needles from his jacket. Then, moving like the gentle ape of a man that he was, he pulled her toward him with a surprising tenderness. She leaned into his face, breathing in the rich salt-smell of his skin, tart with the scent of the pines. She nuzzled his lips with her own, then slowly, slowly slid her tongue between his lips. He grunted, and she knew she had roused him, but still he restrained himself.

For a moment she imagined the heat of her husband's gaze upon her, and her body quivered in pleasure. But then the feeling was gone, and all she could sense was Rob, salt smell and pine smell, the hardness of his body pressing against her, and the burning feeling inside her.

"Now," she whispered, unbuttoning his jeans. She yanked at his pants and underwear and they fell in a heap around his ankles. She touched his hardness and smiled. "Take me now."

Like a dog finally freed from its leash, he attacked her in a frenzy, tearing at her blouse and pants in impatience, pushing her backward hurriedly against a tree. She sighed in pleasure as he entered her, then bit her lip as the bark of the tree dug into her back with his every thrust. The rough stabs of pain from the coarse bark of the tree only made it all the more pleasurable. She closed her eyes, losing herself in the pounding rhythm, finally feeling alive in a way her husband had never been able to show her.

There could be any number of reasons for including a scene such as the one above in a novel. Perhaps Moira is a femme fatale who will later try to talk Rob into murdering her husband. Or maybe Moira is trapped in a loveless marriage and has low self-esteem, and feels that these illicit encounters are her "revenge" on her husband. There could be any number of other reasons for this scene to belong in a novel. However, the rationale for this scene is not to "sex up" a novel.

How Not to Write a Love Scene or Sex Scene

Many beginning writers are so overwhelmed by the intimacy, eroticism and personal nature of a love scene or a sex scene that they retreat to either of two unacceptable extremes: great scenic distance, which records amorous activities with the passive eye of the camera, or pornography, which wallows in lust to the exclusion of all other emotions and exists merely to titillate the reader.

The first choice makes the scene sound like a dispassionate list of physical actions: "Nate embraced Mary, kissing her deeply. He cupped one of her breasts in one hand and began unbuttoning her blouse with the other. As he stripped her, she squirmed and danced in excitement under his touch. He slipped her slacks down around her legs and began fondling her bare buttocks…"

We're asleep. How about you?

The second choice, pornography, is just as distant but much more graphic or even obscene. Here Nate does not merely enter Mary, he "thrusts his burning dick into her wet, pulsating pussy." The words actually interfere with meaning, rather than adding to it. This writing is usually rather painful to read and is often perceived as being just plain crude or even disgusting, or at best out of place. (Note that some of your characters may use obscene words in dialogue. That will tell us about their background and personalities. Remember, though, that a little obscenity goes a long way.)

In a pornographic scene, we have no idea what the two people in the scene are feeling or thinking, much less what they are feeling or thinking about each other, beyond lust. The scene exists merely to deliver sexual content. If this is the case, ask yourself if you really need to write the scene. What does it add to the novel? To the characters?

Scene and Narrative Exercise Four

Objective: To craft an effective sex scene

Eighteen-year-old Don Russell has just finished basic training. He has discovered that he, among all of his buddies, is the only virgin, at least according to them. He has kept his virginity and his shyness around women a secret, however.

Don is on leave for the next week. Convinced that he is missing out on something important and that it is time for him to stop being a child instead of a man, he becomes determined to lose his virginity.

He returns home to Beth, the girl who has always had a crush on him, and drives her out one night to beautiful Rainbow Lake, a six-pack of beer in the back seat. Don tells her that he has missed her. He also implies—untruthfully—that he thinks he might be in love with her.

Write what happens next.

Suspense

Suspense, or the art of keeping the reader wondering what will happen next, is a quality that builds up throughout the novel, from scene to scene. Scenes may build on each other to create suspense, adding pressure on the character to make a decision or take action.

Suspense is not just for murder dramas, police novels, espionage stories and the like; suspense is an integral part of virtually every successful conventional novel. If the reader is truly caught up in the plot of a novel, he'll ask himself "I wonder what will happen next" throughout the novel. He'll care about the major characters and long to find out what becomes of them. Such a longing is a basic facet of human nature, and the wise writer will take advantage of it. Novels which are strongly driven by suspense are called "pageturners," and while not all novels will be filled with suspense, they will still make use of it.

The word "suspense" comes from a Latin word meaning to hang in the air, to be suspended between heaven and earth. We define suspense as the reader's sensation that something is about to happen. It may be something pleasant, but more likely it is something dangerous, frightening or challenging. In effect, the reader is often left hanging, not knowing at a given moment just what is going to happen to the main characters. It is this sensation of not knowing which creates the slightly frightening but somehow pleasantly chilling feeling of suspense.

The careful writer will plant clues throughout his novel to create this sense of suspense. Some will be as subtle as a moment of hesitation…others will be as obvious as a prairie fire and the fear and uncertainty of its outcome.

For instance, in *Lolita*, by Vladamir Nabokov, the reader is kept in a constant state of suspense regarding whether or not the young girl, Lolita, will stay with her stepfather, Humbert, who is obsessed with her budding sexuality. These two are forever on the move, running from another man who seeks Lolita's favors. Humbert receives letters hinting that someone knows of his unsavory relationship with Lolita, letters which put pressure on Humbert to do something and arouse further suspense in the reader as he tries to guess, What will Humbert do?

Such suspense causes the action to rise, and the characters to react, respond, grow and change—with tragic results, in Humbert's case.

Here's another example. In Flannery O'Connor's brilliant short story, *Good Country People*, the young, one-legged, rather unlikable female protagonist meets a traveling salesman. Her intentions are clear: She wants an affair. But the young man's plans are not so clear. Finding out what they are—and how they conflict with hers—form the plot of the story, and the reader is nearly torn apart by suspense as these two climb up to a loft in a barn. The resolution of the story is completely different from what the reader anticipates. Here O'Connor builds suspense not by adding information to pique the curiosity, like Humbert's letters, but by concealing information.

And yet another, theoretical example: A middle-aged woman with a large family is providing a home for her beloved father. When he begins acting bizarrely, she has him evaluated and discovers he is in the early stages of dementia. She begins an emotional journey to answer the question of what to do about her father. As his behavior becomes more peculiar and threatening, suspense increases and the stakes become higher. The reader realizes that, if the woman makes the wrong choice, she may be putting her children in jeopardy.

One more example, and we'll leave you alone!

In H.P. Lovecraft's classic horror story, *Rats in the Walls*, Lovecraft dwells on the protagonist's fascination with phantom rats which appear to be infesting his ancestral mansion. While the main focus of the story is on scenes involving the rats and their spectral appearances, Lovecraft also refers to the protagonist's peculiar ancestors and hints that they might have been involved in bizarre, even murderous activities. Lovecraft thus cleverly focuses the reader's attention on the rats, while inserting secondary but unsettling information about the protagonist's background. In the grim resolution, we discover the rats are only a blind for the real horror: the fact that the protagonist's ancestors were cannibals, and that he has inherited this trait. Thus suspense builds on two levels: 1) the need to get to the bottom of "this rat business," and 2) the aching desire to understand the secrets of the protagonist's heritage and how it has affected him. The reader discovers in the end that the narrator has been telling us his story from a mental institution.

Scene and Narrative Exercise Five

*Objective: To add suspense to story concepts and to write
a short story*

Part 1

Here are some brief outlines of short stories. Currently, these scenarios have little or no sense of suspense, and ultimately the resolutions of each sound flat and dull. Make suggestions for how you would increase suspense for the reader in each case. Ask yourself what is missing in each scenario. What mystery is the reader trying to solve? What might happen to put pressure on the protagonist?

We've included our thoughts on the first case to provide an example.

1. A father, as he is dying, gives a ring to his grown son, telling the young man that the ring is worthless but has a lot of sentimental value. The old man dies, and the son carelessly loses the ring.

To increase suspense, the son might discover the true worth of the ring and go on a search to find it within a short time frame to gain his inheritance. How does he feel now after losing such a valuable possession?

Now suggest ways to add suspense to these story concepts:

2. An attorney successfully defends a man accused of a heinous crime.
3. A young woman writes an angry letter to her fiancé, who is away at war, then discovers some information which convinces her that he is blameless. She destroys the letter.
4. A man and his family, traveling on vacation, pick up a young hitchhiker who leaves them a day later. They find out that he is a serial murderer.

5. A member of a terrorist group guards an American captive for two weeks, is then told to free him and does so.

6. A young man murders his kind-hearted grandfather, then inexplicably confesses the murder to the police.

7. Two space explorers land on a distant planet, expecting to encounter alien life. Instead they find their deceased relatives, miraculously recovered and in good health. The explorers return to earth with a cure for death.

8. A boy is left in the care of a cruel governess who virtually ... prisoner in his house. His only relief is ... with his ferret, kept in a cage in the stables. He fantasizes the ferret is really the spirit of a powerful protector of children. At last his parents return from a prolonged journey, realize the nature of the situation and dismiss the governess.

9. A young man drives a busload of children to camp every day, regaling them with stories about a great hero and his brave pet wolf. One day the man tells the children he has just broken up with his fiancée, and refuses to tell any more stories.

10. Two desperate con-men kidnap the young son of a wealthy businessman. The child is so sweet that the men decide to return him and drop their ransom demands.

Part 2

Outline a short story based on any one of the above scenarios, being sure to incorporate your suggestions for increasing suspense.

Part 3

If you feel up to it, write a short story based on your outline or on any of the ten scenarios. Be sure to consider the element of suspense, putting pressure on your protagonist and keeping the reader guessing as to the direction or resolution of the plot.

Setting the Pace

In writing, as in running, pace refers to how quickly or slowly the object in question—a novel, or a runner—is progressing. Successful long-distance runners pace themselves during a race so that they do not expend all their energies early and find themselves "out of gas" at the end of the race.

Likewise, the writer will also find it necessary to increase or decrease the speed, or pace, of his novel, depending on the reaction he wishes to elicit from the reader and the nature of the story he is writing. In general, the pace of the writing equals the rate at which events occur in the story, and the emphasis placed on each. Although one should avoid a novel that has no pace but "full speed ahead," the faster the pace, the easier it is to read a novel. As the novel heads toward its resolution, pace often increases as earlier parts of the story "drop into place" for the reader, pointing to a logical conclusion. For instance, after hundreds of pages of slowly-building tension, the novel *Moby Dick* seems to sprout legs in its final chapters and dash toward a tragic confrontation with the white whale.

How to Increase Pace and When to Do So

The pace in any given scene of a novel can range from blindingly fast and furious to glacially slow and ponderous, depending on what the writer is trying to do. If the writer wants to depict any exciting event, such as a chase scene, a sports contest, a battle of the wills, an attack, or other dramatic scene, he can increase pace. He'll do this by using short sentences, short words, and little or no dialogue. A love scene, with its long, breathless prose is a major exception to this rule of thumb. Minor events will seem to pile up or "boxcar" on each other as a hunter, for example, sees his quarry, sets off after it, loses sight of it, regains sight, fires, misses, and sets off after his prey, only to become hopelessly lost in the woods. Here's an example of such an action scene, written at a very fast pace:

> Both dogs began barking. Skraggs saw the big raccoon not thirty yards away. The critter looked up in surprise and dashed into the underbrush. Belle and Barney gave chase, yelping as they ran. Skraggs stumbled along behind them and shouted, "Seek! Seek!" The brambles tore as his clothes but he pushed on. Suddenly he heard the hounds baying. *They've treed 'im!* he thought. But when he broke into a clearing, he cursed his luck. The dogs had treed a 'coon, all right—a little female with a broken forepaw. The big bastard had given them all the slip.

Not all scenes which demand a fairly fast pace should be written at a breakneck pace, of course, and some scenes using a lot of dialogue will also move quite quickly. The pace depends to a large extent on what is being revealed in the scene and how much suspense is being built up.

One way to increase pace is by increasing suspense. To do this, the writer can increase tension on the characters. For example, what would happen if the big raccoon in the section above were rabid and the hunter were trying to kill it before it infected anyone? This would change the hunter's sport into serious business, which would in turn increase the need for his success and underscore his failure. Such a sense of pressure makes the pace seem to move faster.

Speed of movement from one point to the next within a scene defines pace, though the pace may vary from slow to fast within any scene. Sometimes the pace will begin at a relaxed rate and quickly accelerate as the reader approaches a climatic action or image.

Besides using physical action and increasing suspense, a writer can pick up the pace of fiction by increasing the intensity of emotions. Characters' intense feelings of passion, rage, fear and so on will make pace appear to speed up, since the reader will be more deeply drawn into the plight of the characters.

Scene and Narrative Exercise Six

Objective: To increase pace

Part 1

The following passage would read better if the pace were faster. Jot down notes on what you would do to increase the pace here, and why.

> Johnston guided the big van skillfully down the steep mountain road. As he approached a sharp curve, Johnston pressed down on the brake and was surprised to find it mushy and unresponsive. His foot went right to the floor, but the van slowed down only a little, and he just managed to guide it around the curve, the tires screeching and pebbles spraying out over the side of the cliff.
>
> *That was close*, thought Johnston. He had once raced Grand Prix cars in road races in Germany and knew every trick in the trade about driving on curves and slopes. He was proud of his driving abilities, and especially partial to his nickname, Ice, earned because of his confidence and coolness under extreme pressure.
>
> When he tried the brakes again he found that they were completely gone and quite unable to stop his van. He pulled the emergency brake, risking the destruction of the transmission, but there was no response at all. The van continued rocketing down the hillside at a great rate of speed which, Johnston quickly calcu-

lated, would soon propel the vehicle out of control, either off the cliff on one side or into the mountain wall on the other. Maintaining an icy calmness while struggling to control the van and rack his brains for a strategy, Johnston approached a hairpin curve.

At the same time he wondered who could have sabotaged his van. The only people besides himself who ever worked on his vehicles were Blake, his mechanic, and Pete, his son-in-law. Johnston could not imagine gentle Blake or Pete, who was like a son to him, tampering with the van in such a deadly fashion, but he knew the problems weren't due to poor maintenance. Both brakes had failed, and he didn't know how such a thing could happen, short of dirty work.

Part 2

Read the passage about Ice Johnston again. Ho-hum. Johnston seems to be speeding to certain death, but he's the only thing that's speeding. Even though this is potentially a nail-biting, edge-of-the-seat scene, the reader is at risk of falling asleep at the wheel before Ice Johnston can rectify the situation.

You no doubt pointed out that Johnston's memories of his racing days and his musings over who might have sabotaged the van diverted the reader from the action and slowed down the pace. Repetition, long, lackadaisical sentences and a certain lack of emotion in the language kept the reader at arm's length and thus made this passage a slow read.

Keeping all this in mind, rewrite the passage about Ice Johnston so that it is as fast-paced as Johnston's out-of-control van.

How to Slow Pace and When to Do So

Just as we quickened the pace with short sentences, short words, suspense and action, we can use longer words and sentences, more leisurely description, calm or restful scenes and moments of reflection or quiet thought to slow down a scene. These are all signals to the reader to relax and be thoughtfully receptive; to take a breather from the action of the story. As long as the writer manages to hold the reader's interest, this "breather" may be as long as the author desires.

Slowing down the pace is a valid way to vary the pace of the novel, especially following fast-paced action scenes or scenes involving intense emotions. Slow-paced scenes involving introspection, reflection and recollection add depth to characters and allow readers to understand the characters better. A character enjoying a tranquil moment or mulling over a problem, two characters involved in an intimate conversation, or a character's recollection or description of an important item or place are all potential scenarios that will benefit from a slower pace.

Scene and Narrative Exercise Seven

Objective: To identify pace

Based on the following descriptions of various incidents, note which are best suited for a faster pace (F) and which probably require a slower pace (S). Which might conceivably require a mixture of both (M)?

1. Andrea Skyeagle, a young Sioux, returns to her grandmother's home on the reservation after dropping out of her university studies. Andrea's grandmother is waiting for her at the train station; she has brought a pick-up truck and Andrea's old pet sheepdog.

2. Alex, a wealthy lawyer with a mistress, has just joined his unsuspecting wife in the kitchen after she has put the kids to bed. He is feeling guilty and intends to tell her all.

3. Travis, a Yankee scout, rides around a bend in the road and sees three Rebel soldiers blocking his path.

4. Grandfather tells Josh, his youngest grandson, who is nine years old, that Josh's grandmother is dying.

5. Lady Helena, the young ward of a Norman knight, has stolen out of her protector's castle one night and gone for a walk in the woods. She is gathering herbs by moonlight when she suddenly hears the howl of a wolf, too close for comfort.

6. Captain Oryxt, commander of the Galactic Union vessel Astral, is amused by a cadet's question about the starship and proceeds to tell the young woman the history of the much-used vessel during a lull in their voyage.

7. Dirk Simpson, cowhand-for-hire, rides into Prairie, Montana one afternoon and is surprised to find a half-grown colt with a ragged rope halter on the outskirts of

town. Acting on a whim, he shoots his pistol, frightening the beast. The colt takes off and Dirk follows,
intending to let the horse lead him to the nearby ranch
from which, he assumes, it has strayed.

8. Waking up the day after his wedding, which took place
   the evening of VE day, Sergeant Hank Armstrong begins
   to wonder if he has done the right thing or not in
   marrying Lillian.

9. Special investigator Betty Wolfe arrives at what she
   believes to be the scene of a murder. It isn't...yet. She
   has mistakenly gone to the wrong house and walked in
   on a husband beating his wife into a bloody pulp.

Flashbacks

One of the most effective ways of slowing pace can be to introduce a flashback. A flashback is a character's memory of a past event, perhaps from his childhood, his college years, his military service, his first marriage, his first big job, and so on. The flashback not only serves as a good way to give the reader crucial information about the character's background without sounding obvious or contrived, but can also provide a "break" in the faster pace of the story. Of course, a flashback may also be used to add tension to a story, if the character is recalling a particularly stressful incident from his past. In mysteries, flashback recollections sometimes provide the solution to crimes and enigmas.

Flashbacks may be rendered in either scene or narrative, but the most common kind of flashback may be the narrative scene. It is important not to let flashback scenes become so long and rambling that they take precedence over the main story.

Although flashbacks are useful, new writers frequently face several problems when trying to create a successful flashback.

1. *Beginning with a flashback*—It makes no sense to do this, since a flashback is essentially a memory, and there must be a character with a background before there is a memory of a background. Establish setting, character and conflict before introducing a flashback, and use flashbacks sparingly.

2. *Creating a flashback within a flashback*—One recollection at a time is enough. If your protagonist remembers his college years, then in flashback recalls his 9th-grade sweetheart, and subsequently his first day in school, your reader will be heartily confused as to what is happening when.

3. *Failing to get into and out of a flashback*—Flashbacks don't just happen. The writer must have his character respond to some memory trigger, which in turn elicits an appropriate memory. The taste of Madeline cakes, for instance, causes Proust to recall his childhood in *Remembrance of Things Past*. Once the flashback is finished, the character must return to "present time." This can be accomplished by letting your character respond to some sensory stimulus in present time—someone speaking to him, perhaps, or the smell of bacon frying or a glance at the clock on the wall or some other indication of the "real" world.

4. *Referring to flashbacks in the text*—One does not "flashback" on a memory; one remembers, recalls or recollects a past event. A flashback is a literary technique, not something real people do. Do not make the mistake of one novice wordsmith who used a separate heading to label a flashback "Flashback on John's Early Life in Tennessee." This only draws attention to the fact that the reader is reading an artificial construct instead of participating in an alternate reality.

5. *Writing a very long flashback, or trying to tell a story in flashback*—A flashback is usually fairly brief. That is because the flashback itself is not the story; it is only a method of providing information critical to the story. The flashback also provides us with a closer look into the personality of the character and lets us see what events have shaped his life in certain ways. If you are trying to write a story in flashback, you probably really want to write a memoir, or fictional memoir. As mentioned before, flashbacks regarding recent events can also provide clues or resolutions to mysteries. For ex-

Scene and Narrative Exercise Eight

Objective: To recognize effective flashbacks

Here are three brief flashbacks. In your opinion, which two are working properly and which one is not? What is effective about the ones that work? Why isn't the other effective? How might you rewrite the unsuccessful flashback to make it stronger?

1. Laura thought about the hard life she had led. Not only did she grow up in poverty in the hills of West Virginia, she had married a truck driver when she was just sixteen and had four children before he ran off with the town tramp and never came back. She had gotten a job in the medical supply factory while her mother looked after the kids, but it was hard, boring work and she despised it. Laura started taking high school equivalency classes at night, and she soon earned her G.E.D., passing with top honors. Even so she had never believed she would ever go to college. Even when she was little she had never dreamed of that.

2. An 18-wheeler drove into the parking lot of the truckstop, and Laura closed her eyes. She didn't want to look at it; it might be Harry's truck. Whenever she saw big trucks she thought of Harry and all the pain he had caused her when he left her alone, a frightened 19-year-old with four babies. But it was too late—she thought of him anyway, the first time she had seen him. She'd known at that moment he was going to marry her and take her away from the Blue Ridge hill country and backbreaking work in the fields of her father's farm. He was only 20 years old, tall and good looking. He'd been happy back

then and never touched a drop of liquor.

3. My mother spoke to me—something about starting dinner—but I didn't listen to her. I never listened to her, not even as a small child. Instead of getting up and fetching pots and pans and pulling food from the fridge, I sat back and remembered the day I stopped listening. I had been only four years old, and I had done something wrong; I think I had gotten my clothes dirty in the garden. My mother told me to pull down my drawers right there in the open, outside, because she was going to take a hairbrush to my bottom and she didn't care who saw how nasty I was. Well, I'd been paddled a lot at age four, but never in front of the neighbors, so I just ran inside the house and hid in my room. She paddled me anyway, but not outdoors. I had won.

Transitions

Once you've crafted an effective scene, what do you do with it? Why, leave it and move on to the next, of course. But how? More importantly, how do you take your reader with you?

The answer is, with a transition.

A transition is a bridge, almost always in narrative form, that takes the reader from one scene to another, from chapter to chapter, or even from paragraph to paragraph. Transitions allow the story to flow smoothly. While it may seem to flow well enough to you, remember that you are very familiar with the plot and characters. Remember, too, that your readers will not have the advantage of outlines, synopses, notes or any other kind of roadmap for negotiating your story. They have only what's on the page before them. Therefore, appropriate, effective transitions are essential.

What happens if a writer simply "cuts" from one scene to another, just as a movie cuts from scene to scene? The reader may be confused and angry if he cannot follow the story line or if he feels as if he is being bounced around like a tennis ball. At best, your reader may feel uncertain about critical information: 1) Where is the new scene taking place? 2) How much time has elapsed between scenes? 3) Who is in the new scene? 4) Is there a specific reason those characters are in this scene? Depending on the scene, transitions may not, however, need to address all these points.

Types of Transitions

There are at least four types of transitions. They are:

1. *Narrative passages*—Narrative descriptions of the passage of time can move a reader from Easter morning to

New Year's Eve, or from the birth of a child to his second birthday. ("The seasons passed quickly for Becky, and before she quite knew what had hit her she was in the last month of pregnancy.") Writers also use narrative descriptions to establish a new scene with a new setting. ("Her grandmother's house was exactly how she had imagined it, with worn porch steps and blue-shuttered windows and a pair of friendly, rumpled-looking pine trees that seemed to reach out for her in welcome.") Such narrative passages are usually used to "set" the beginning of a chapter.

2. *Bridge words*—Transitional words such as "meanwhile," "nevertheless," and "later" are the easiest form of transition, but are usually not very effective at bridging the gap between scenes or chapters. Transitional phrases— "Meanwhile, in the harbor section of the city"..."Two hours later, back at Rex's apartment"—are a little stronger.

3. *Transitional sentences*—This is one of the best ways to create a solid bridge between scenes or chapters. Here's a simplistic example, used to help a new character enter a scene:

> Darla sat down at her usual table at the Hoedown Cafe to wait for Danny. She hadn't the slightest doubt that he'd show up speechless with amazement or admiration or both.
>
> He arrived about half an hour later, slapping snow off his overcoat. "I can't believe it! You were right!" he gasped by way of greeting. "The Penguins beat New York 7 to 2. You're really something!"

Now read this without the third sentence. Awkward, isn't it? Danny just seems to "appear" in the scene by magic. Oddly enough, this sort of truncated writing is very common among new writers, though the awkward gap is usually found between scenes.

4. *Transitional paragraphs*—Kissing cousin of the transitional sentence, the transitional paragraph is useful when forming connections between scenes or chapters when the gulf in time, place or circumstance from one section to the next is very wide or complex. Some transitions may even require several paragraphs, or even an entire scene.

Unlike a movie, a novel does not "cut" to new scenes. It cannot effectively do so, because writing has no visual clues to help the audience recognize a new situation and adjust to the new scene. In a novel, the narrative transition provides the information the reader needs to comfortably segue from one distinct place or time to another.

Scene and Narrative Exercise Nine

Objective: To create transitions

Rewrite this passage, creating a transition between the two large paragraphs, each of which depicts a different scene. Get James from thinking about Sean to the point where he is searching for the boy. You will need to get him from the classroom to his car. Consider why he is looking for Sean and what he plans to do or say to the teen. Can you form an effective transition using one sentence, or do you need a paragraph? Either solution is perfectly viable; the shorter transition will be more difficult to write.

James began grading papers, but his mind was on Sean. Why hadn't the boy shown up in class? According to Ms. Parker, he hadn't gone to his music class, either. Was he just playing hooky...or was he with that Roth kid again, down on Powell Street where the toughs and pushers hung out?

James drove slowly down the wide avenue, inspecting each teenager he saw, searching for Sean. At last he found him, standing on a street corner, his hands in his pockets, a lit cigarette all but falling from his lips. When James drove up to him and hailed him, Sean stared, dropped his cig and ran.

Damn! thought James.

Cool Down

Scenes, narrative and the combination of both are the basic fabrics of a novel. Joining them together into a flowing, easy-to-read piece of writing takes ability; keeping the story progressing while varying pace and creating suspense is an even greater challenge. In a way, a novel is like a quilt, carefully pieced together from different types of cloth. If the stitches are fine enough and the skill great enough, the quilt will appear seamless. So it is with writing.

9

Pep Talk: Dialogue

*Speak clearly, if you speak at all; carve every
word before you let it fall.*

—Oliver Wendell Holmes

People talk to each other. In everyday life, it's called speech.
In writing, it's called dialogue.

Dialogue is a fact of life that every novelist must get used to,
whether she likes to write dialogue or not, since it is a key aspect
of many scenes. In fact, scenes using effective dialogue are
usually the strongest, most powerful parts of a novel. In addi-

tion, resolutions frequently take place through dialogue as rivals confront each other, secrets are revealed, and promises are made.

So why do so many writers shy away from dialogue?

For one thing, it's not all that easy to write dialogue that sounds like natural conversation but still advances plot and/or character. If dialogue sounds wooden, awkward or inappropriate, the reader will stop "buying into" the fictional world the writer is trying to create. The characters spouting the dialogue will no longer appear "real," and the entire scene, or perhaps the entire novel, will look contrived, manipulated, and artificial.

Dialogue with a Purpose

Fictional dialogue has a different purpose than the speech we hear every day. People talk for many reasons, including to pass time, make a social gesture, or simply fill up the silences in their lives. But fictional characters always speak for a specific reason, and everything they say has a specific purpose. Some of these purposes include:

1. Revealing the personalities of the characters, through their word choice, topics and the ways they express themselves.
2. Revealing plot complications or areas of conflict.
3. Revealing characters' reactions to important events.
4. Describing POV characters.
5. Rendering tense, critical communications—confrontations, confessions, and the like—in a dramatic, realistic way.

Because dialogue has so many important purposes, it cannot

sound like "real speech," although, paradoxically, it must give the impression of being real speech.

Read the following section of so-called "realistic" dialogue, written by a beginning writer.

> "Morning, Judy," said Liz. "Going shopping?"
>
> "Yes, Liz. Big sale as Nordstroms today."
>
> "No kidding! Can I go with you, Judy? I need a new pair of black slacks."
>
> "Sure you can come, Liz," Judy replied. "We can have lunch at The Winter Garden."

What is the purpose of this dialogue? Have we learned much about either woman, other than both like to shop? Have we learned anything about their personalities or backgrounds? Does the dialogue have a reason for being, or is it just there for the sake of adding dialogue? If it's not adding to the development of plot, character or setting, it should be omitted.

Notice that this dialogue is very scenic. Point of view is not attached to any character, but simply thrown at the reader. As a result, it is difficult to tell anything about the personality of either woman.

Worse yet, this dialogue doesn't sound realistic at all. Instead it sounds wooden and contrived, largely because it has no purpose. Also, people do not address each other by name very often in speech.

Dialogue Exercise One

Objective: To create dialogue

Rewrite the following narrative passage in dialogue, choosing either Ralph's or Maureen's POV. What might be the purpose of the characters' dialogue here? What can you reveal about them through their dialogue?

> Maureen tried to build a campfire in the clearing, but Ralph kept finding fault with it. He thought the kindling she was using was too big and scolded her for not building a fire ring of stones around the fire first. Maureen countered that he should have helped her right from the beginning, or built the fire himself if he had such strong opinions about it. Ralph was quick to point out that he had been busy setting up the tent, a crucial task. Maureen asked how much less crucial a fire was, considering the cold, but Ralph has already begun piling stones around her arrangement of sticks and no longer seemed to be listening to her.

Two Errors to Avoid When Writing Dialogue

Beginning writers are often plagued by two serious problems when crafting dialogue: Either they write 1) scripts, or 2) heavy-handed dialogue.

Scripts

Have you ever seen—or written—pages of dialogue virtually unbroken by any narrative? Such dialogues look like scripts from a play or screenplay and are usually a good indication that the writer is thinking in terms of a movie, not a novel. The dialogue between Liz and Judy in the beginning of this chapter is a script; so is the following:

> "You knew Carlotti, didn't you?" Carson asked.
>
> "Sure, a little. I met him at college and worked with him for a while at Remington Industries. We were never close, though."
>
> "Did you see him at the Worthingtons' party last Saturday?"
>
> "Yes," Julia said, hesitating. "He asked me if he could get me a drink. I told him I just wanted sparkling water, and he brought me some."
>
> "When was that?"
>
> "Well, around ten, I guess. I left shortly after that, because my sitter called and told me my little girl wasn't feeling well."
>
> "So you didn't know Carlotti had been shot until after you got home?"
>
> "That's right, the next morning, in fact. I

heard about it on the news while I was fixing breakfast."

Since this is a sort of interrogation scene, you'd expect a lot of dialogue, which is fine. What's missing is enhancing narrative and an attached point of view, which allows the POV character to think about the situation. By accessing the protagonist's thoughts and feelings, the reader can understand how the character reacts to any given conversation. Such reactions allow the reader to form an idea of the POV character's personality. A sense of movement or life, or any indication of personality is missing from the scriptlike dialogue. There is a purpose, but there is no texture.

Sometimes the dialogue is not even properly attributed, that is, we don't know which character is speaking at any given time. This is most confusing, especially if three or more characters are speaking. The occasional use of attributions ("Marissa said," "Frank shouted") are not only helpful but probably necessary to prevent confusion. The best word to use for attributing dialogue is the most simple one: "said." "Speaking verbs" such as yelled, rasped, murmured, whispered, sighed, and so on, provide welcome variation but should not be overused.

More serious is the lack of beats within "scripted" dialogue. Beats are minor actions or bits of stage business—running one's hand through one's hair or stooping to gently scratch a dog's ears—rendered in narrative, which make the speakers come alive and give the impression that they exist beyond the words they are saying. Beats also give a sense of order and organization, and provide the illusion of reality. The dialogue between Carson and Julia is completely devoid of beats. Here are some examples of how beats can bring a dialogue to life; the line in parentheses shows what character trait is being revealed in the beat.

"You knew Carlotti, didn't you?" Carson asked, thrusting his face forward about two inches from Julia's. (Carson is aggressive and brash.)

"I heard about his death on the radio the next morning." Julia twirled the ring on her pinkie finger round and round, and Carson could see the skin underneath the ring was bright pink. (Julia is nervous, and Carson knows it.)

"I don't think you should see the body," Carson said softly. "He's already been identified. He took three shots to the head, you know, and six to the chest." Carson flinched as his stomach twisted into a knot at the memory of Carlotti's shattered corpse. (Carson may be an experienced investigator, but he is human enough to be moved by Carlotti's grisly death and to be wary of letting Julia view the body.)

"There isn't any reason for us to continue this discussion, is there?" Julia retrieved her cigarette from the ashtray and took a long drag, her hand shaking all the while. *She's hiding something*, Carson thought. (Her shaking hand reveals her discomfort and gives the lie to the notion that "there's no reason to continue talking.")

If you observe two people conversing, you will notice that much information is given that is not spoken. The posture of the speakers, what they do with their hands, and other aspects of their body English will say much about the actual meaning of their words. For instance, the speaker who comes on strong with his language but does not look the person he's addressing in the face is hiding something. Be sure to give these important clues to the reader.

Remember too that a script is an obvious artifice. A long dialogue devoid of narrative will appear unrealistic and contrived. Keep in mind that your POV character will react to conversation with thoughts and feelings, which the reader should be privy to. Be aware, too, that life goes on around people as they are speaking, and your POV character may notice leaves falling or children laughing while the conversation takes place. These details can add up to create an impression of realism and a persuasive replica of real speech and real life.

Dialogue Exercise Two

Objective: To enhance dialogue

Rewrite the following tense conversation with appropriate beats, in Mrs. Winslow's POV. Create details about characters, setting and so forth at will, as needed. Notice how much more suspenseful the scene is with the addition of thoughts, movements, and physical reactions such as glances, hand gestures, and facial expressions. Don't forget the effect of the setting too, and the characters' reactions to it. Is a clock ticking in the silence? Is the wind blowing? Is snow or rain falling? Is the room lit by a single hurricane lamp? Use your imagination to create the scene. Remember to render the scene entirely in Mrs. Winslow's point of view; the reader is aware of no one's thoughts but hers.

"Lady, put down that rifle. It's loaded. You're liable to hurt someone."

"I'm liable to hurt you, you mean," she said. "Now back up right out of the door and out of this house. If you don't get on your horse and leave, I swear I'll kill you."

"I don't believe it, Miz Winslow," he chuckled. "You're just trying to scare me. Look, why don't you put down the gun and—I tell you what—you and me'll just have a cup of coffee together and talk for a little bit. If you want to tell me where your husband is, that's fine. If you don't, that's fine. I'll leave of my own accord."

"I don't trust you for one single moment, Mr. Granger," she said. "You see, you want Sam dead, and I want him to live. I can't afford to trust you."

Heavy-Handed Dialogue

The second most common error in writing dialogue is the mistake of loading the reader down with information, usually information which characters already know. The effect is to leave the reader feeling as if he is being manipulated, as if the writer feels she must explain every nuance of the story to the doltish reader.

Sometimes this information is extraneous, but sometimes it is important; if it's vital, it can be rendered in narrative, often in the form of the POV character's thoughts and memories.

The following—the beginning of a poorly-written crime novel—is an example of bad dialogue that puts too much emphasis on information that is obvious to the characters.

> "Ben, did you get the orders from the boss?" asked Harry, once Ben had settled himself inside the Jaguar.
>
> "Yeah, the plans have changed. Instead of kidnapping Hal Diamond's wife, now we gotta waste her."
>
> "Did he say why?" Harry lit a cigarette and puffed away in agitation. "She's a beautiful woman, isn't she? And she's got those four kids to take care of, including that little girl with…what is it?"
>
> "Cystic fiber-something."
>
> "Yeah. I dunno, that's gonna be a hard one. Well, did he say why?"
>
> Ben nodded. "Remember what the boss said during the last meeting? That the broad had seen Harper rub out Feinstein, the guy that sang to the cops? At first the boss just wanted to give

Diamond a good scare and make him back away from prosecution, but things are different now. She's got to be permanently sidetracked, just like Bloom and that Applegate woman." Ben smiled suddenly and patted Harry's shoulder. "Don't worry, Harry. You've got nerves of steel. Remember how you took out that Ames character last week? There wasn't a sound and you didn't leave a clue. Just do the same thing again."

"Well, it's still going to be hard," said Harry, blowing a smoke ring. "I keep thinking of that kid."

In the dialogue above, hit-men Harry and Ben seem to rehash old business that both of them would know about but the reader wouldn't—Mrs. Diamond's appearance and family life, her observation of Feinstein's death, the original reason for the planned kidnapping, three other assassinations Harry has committed and his "nerves of steel." The real purpose of this conversation is to inform Harry of a change in plans: Mrs. Diamond must die. The rest of the details are exposition for the benefit of the reader and should not be presented in dialogue between these two well-informed characters.

In order to avoid stating the obvious and still develop Harry's character and increase tension, the writer could try including some of the details in narrative form instead of in dialogue. For example, Harry could think about Mrs. Diamond and her little girl; he could remember how easy it had been to kill Ames; he could think of the reputation he had as a cold-blooded killer and wonder why he was so hesitant now to carry out his duties.

Heavy-handed dialogue is an occupational hazard for writers of mysteries, espionage novels, science fiction and period novels; these may all breed many details and interesting past events which the writer may feel obligated to explain to the reader. The writer may think he is doing the reader a service to do so, but he is really contriving and explaining facts to the point that the reader feels tricked or insulted. In nearly every case, it is best to present background information subtly enough so that the reader believes he has uncovered it himself.

Skillful dialogue helps craft the scene, showing us insights into characters and situations. (See the examples in the section on beats.) The background details—far less important than character and conflict development—will come forward somewhere in the story, if they are important.

Dialogue Exercise Three

Objective: To rewrite heavy-handed dialogue

Rewrite this passage from a science fiction story, omitting all heavy-handed dialogue (information the characters would already know). Some of this information is important, though, for creating suspense and tension. Decide what information is important and rework it in narrative form, perhaps as Jake's indirect thoughts. Remember to stay in Jake's POV, or rewrite the entire scene in Hank's POV.

Jake walked across the captain's bridge to his science officer's station. "What have you got, Hank?"

"Well, captain, the scanner, which sends a variety of signals at various wavelengths and bandwidths, shows that the alien ship is in range to send an exploratory team."

"Good, Hank," Jake said and rubbed his chin. "This looks like the ship we've been looking for. The Federation sent us to this quadrant hoping that we could locate this strange vessel, which suddenly appeared on our scanners a week ago."

"Exactly, captain," Hank added excitedly. "This is the vessel that has been emitting a strange, previously unheard of form of cosmic radiation, which was why the Federation was so interested in it in the first place."

"That's right, Hank. Looks like the Federation knew what it was doing when it appointed you science officer after you scored so high on all of your academy exams."

"Ha ha. Just doing my job, captain."

Indirect Discourse

"I see the shoreline now," Ellen said.
Ellen said that she saw the shoreline.

The first sentence above is in direct dialogue; the speaker's exact words are recorded. The second sentence is in indirect dialogue, or indirect discourse; the meaning of the speaker's words are summarized, but she is not quoted directly. Both sentences give the reader the same message, but the former reports what the character said, word for word, while the latter indicates the meaning.

Indirect dialogue allows the writer to intimate the high points of a dialogue without recording every word of a lengthy conversation. In effect, the writer can narrate a conversation, or part of it. This is especially useful for condensing a long conversation which has little results or importance. ("Tom and Elise spent the entire evening discussing the meaning of 'Fellini's Satyricon.'") Indirect discourse also highlights the truly important parts of a conversation, which can be rendered in direct dialogue. ("Tom and Elise spent the entire evening discussing the meaning of 'Fellini's Satyricon.' 'No one but you ever listened so closely to what I had to say,' Tom told her.")

Indirect discourse is not very useful for portraying tense, suspenseful scenes that require at least some direct dialogue. Remember the exercise passage in which Mr. Granger is trying to persuade Mrs. Winslow to put down her rifle? Here is the same passage, taken out of direct dialogue and rewritten in indirect dialogue. Notice how told and distant it sounds. Probably a combination of direct and indirect dialogue would be the best vehicle for this passage.

In as soft a voice as he could muster, Granger

asked Mrs. Winslow to lay the rifle on the table in front of her. It was loaded, he said, and she was going to hurt someone.

She pulled the rifle a little closer to herself, frowned, and informed him that the only person she was liable to hurt was him if he kept pestering her about putting the gun down. Scowling at him fiercely, she demanded that he leave the house and ride away. She'd kill him, she said, if he didn't do as she instructed.

Granger shook his head. He didn't believe that Mrs. Winslow—quiet, friendly Mrs. Winslow—would hurt a gnat, let alone the sheriff of Bluebird County. She had a right to be upset about her husband and the fact that the law was after him, but her threat was probably just a bluff.

Again he gently instructed her to put down the gun and fix them each a cup of coffee. Maybe they could talk for a little bit, he coaxed her. If she wanted to tell him where her husband was, that was fine. If she didn't, he'd just quietly leave of his own accord. As he was speaking, Granger formed a plan: He'd leave if he had to, but ride only a short distance away and wait to see if Mr. Winslow returned to the ranch.

But Mrs. Winslow was not very accommodating. She aimed the rifle square at Granger's chest and said she didn't trust him any further than her big toe. She couldn't afford to trust Granger, she sighed, since he wanted Sam dead and she wanted him alive.

Unless a dialogue is truly revealing, necessary or interesting, try writing it in indirect dialogue. Narrate sections of longer conversations that seem to go on forever without making much impact.

Indirect Thoughts

In writing, a character's direct thoughts are expressed in first person in italics: *If only I had known about David's drinking problem*, Sally thought…*I've got to give the ring back to the sorcerer*, Pippin lamented to himself.

Like indirect dialogue, indirect thoughts are narrative summaries of a character's thoughts in the third person: If only she had known about David's drinking problem, Sally thought…He had to give the ring back to the sorcerer, Pippin told himself. Indirect thoughts are useful, since long strings of italicized direct thoughts are hard to read and soon begin to ramble, like inner monologues.

Sometimes a mixture of the two forms is effective:

> *Maybe I can force the ring off*, Pippin thought.
> He rubbed his hand all day with all manner of
> oils and soaps and potions, but the gold circlet
> clung to his finger still, as if it had made a
> decision to remain and refused to be ousted. It
> didn't belong with him, Pippin realized: That
> was why it was being so stubbornly contrary.
> *I've got to give the ring back to the sorcerer*, Pippin
> lamented to himself.

Indirect thought is very useful for presenting a POV character's long thoughts and musings, or for summing up interior "discussions" which are not important enough to be rendered directly. Presenting a long thought process or parts of that process indirectly allows the writer to avoid the semblance of an inner monologue, a tedious drawback of the first person POV.

Dialogue Exercise Four

Objective: To identify direct and indirect dialogue as well as direct and indirect thoughts

Part 1

Read the following section about Pippin's adventures as he tries to locate Draco, the shape-changing wizard from whom he has stolen the ring on a dare. Mark direct dialogue with the initials DD, indirect dialogue ID, direct thoughts DT and indirect thoughts IT.

"Excuse me, sir, have you seen a wizard in here lately?" asked Pippin, staring straight into the face of the weary barkeep.

The barkeep sighed, leaned over the brightly polished bar and brought his face so close to Pippin's nose that Pippin could smell the man's beery breath. "Wizard, eh?" The man asked if by a wizard Pippin meant a tall, bearded man in a black cape.

Pippin felt his heart begin to beat faster. *He has seen Draco*, he thought. "Yes! When did you see him?" he cried.

The barkeep drew back and began pouring a glass of brandy for a customer. "Haven't seen no one like that at all. Ever," he muttered. As Pippin gazed at the man in confusion, a sly smile crept over the barkeep's lips. Several customers began to laugh out loud and tell each other what a card the old man was.

"It's not a jest," growled Pippin, slamming his right hand down hard on the bar. Too late he

realized that the barkeep and one or two of the
customers had noticed the glittering ring. Pippin quickly slipped his hand into his pocket,
apologized for bothering the keep and explained
that he'd best be leaving.

"Don't go just yet, lad."

Pippin felt a strong hand grip him by the
shoulder. "First tell us what a scruffy imp of a
pup such as yourself is doing with a ring such as
that?"

Pippin looked up at the man and felt his
bones begin to melt in fear. *I'm as good as dead*,
he whimpered to himself. His captor was as tall
as a wall and almost as wide, with a bald head
and no neck to speak of. Behind him, several
men had gathered and begun mumbling about
the ring to themselves.

Pippin knew he had no chance with the
men; he had to leave, but there was only one
way. Stammering some reply about finding the
ring outside an herbalist's shop, Pippin began to
shrug his shoulders and wriggle about in the big
man's grasp.

"Stand still, devil take you!" roared the wall-
man, but Pippin had already worked his way out
of his tunic and was bolting out the door.

He flew through the courtyard, a group of
men hard at his heels. Had they not been drinking, he knew, they would soon have caught him
up, but in their semi-inebriated state they could
only give half-hearted pursuit. About half a mile
from the inn Pippin crawled into a stand of thick

reeds and watched the men mill about, searching for him.

"Can I be of assistance?" asked a soft voice.

Pippin looked down and saw a beautiful black hare lying beside him, its liquid eyes regarding him with great curiosity. He stared at the creature open-mouthed.

"I believe you have something that belongs to me," said the hare, extending its dainty forefoot. "Alas, it will hardly fit me now!"

"Draco!" shouted Pippin, and was instantly aware that he had made a terrible error. *The men. The men have heard me.*

His pursuers stopped their search and began loping toward him with cries of "Found 'im!" "Got 'im!" "The ring is ours!"

Pippin choked out a few words of explanation for the hare, which threw back its head and emitted a sort of strangled laugh. "Well, I suppose you need my assistance," it said.

All at once the hare began to shift and stretch, and right before Pippin's astonished eyes it churned and shimmied and finally transformed into a handsome black horse. "Hop up!" called the horse, stamping his foot.

The men from the inn all drew to a halt, only an arm's length from the stallion's glistening eyes. "Black sorcery!" they cried, and turned to flee. The wall-man paused, his eyes bulging from his face, but before he could utter a word Pippin threw himself on the horse's back and clung to the beast's rippling mane.

"Good day," said the horse in a polite tone of voice, and before Pippin could gather his wits the horse gathered himself and leaped straight over the wall-man. Pippin was certain he would fall, then thought he might not, and before he knew for sure whether he had fallen or not the horse was racing through the forest, weaving in and around the tall pines at amazing speed.

Pippin closed his eyes and gripped the enchanted horse's mane with all his might. *I wonder if Mother will believe all this when I return*, he thought. *If I return.*

Dialogue Exercise Five

Objective: To create a scene using direct and indirect dialogue as well as direct and indirect thoughts

Write a short fictional passage of any sort, 1–2 pages long, using at least three examples of direct dialogue, 2 of indirect dialogue, 1 of direct thought and 2 of indirect thought.

Cool Down

Writing dialogue is one of the most difficult skills to master, largely because it involves a contradiction: How does the writer craft "speech" which sounds natural and realistic, while at the same time makes a dramatic impact and delivers valuable information about characters and plot?

As you go about your everyday life, listen to people speaking. Pay attention not to what they say but how they say it. Do they gesture and change their facial expressions as they speak? Does their body language change depending on their topic of conversation? You may be surprised to discover how much of what writers call "dialogue" is not just speech but other forms of communication, including periods of silence. Ask yourself how you as a writer can translate the intricacies of a human conversation into a written form.

10
Let's Get Physical: Imagery

A writer lives in awe of words for they can be cruel or kind, and they can change their meanings right in front of you. They pick up flavors and odors like butter in a refrigerator.

—John Steinbeck

Of all the literary conventions, imagery and physical description are the most memorable. No doubt you can easily recall your favorite images from literature—the head of a dead pig in William Golding's *The Lord of the Flies*; the lair of the

225

dragon, Smaug, in J.R. Tolkien's *The Hobbit*; the sensuous image of Ishmael covering his hands in ambergris in Melville's *Moby Dick*; the pathetic image of a homely woman in James Joyce's story, "Clay." We use our imagination to imitate reality and create an alternate reality, populated by images which in turn are modeled on people, objects and experiences from our lives.

In your writing, you should also strive to create memorable images or scenes using images that ring so true to reality that they linger in the reader's mind. They may be beautiful, elegant, heart-warming, shocking, ghastly, horrifying or tragic, but so vivid and fresh that they are not easily forgotten.

What if you are writing fantasy or science fiction? Can your images ring true to life if you are describing dragons, aliens, the denizens of an underwater Atlantis or the like? The answer is, of course! The old admonition to "write what you know" probably sprang from the mind of someone with little or no imagination. That doesn't excuse the writer from doing necessary research and careful preparation, however, so that his fantasy worlds will appear "realistic" within their own context.

How does one create powerful images? In this chapter we'll work on doing just that.

Sensual Description

One of the most effective ways to communicate with the reader is to appeal to his five senses: Let him see, hear, taste, smell and touch what you are talking about so he can experience your writing vicariously. The more vivid an image—the more senses it brings into play—the more memorable it is.

As you read the following passage, ask yourself how the writer is using physical imagery to create memorable description. What does the description say about the POV character?

Abby was gazing at the sunlit moor when a red fox trotted in front of her. Why, it doesn't see me, she thought. It didn't scent her, either. Such a beautiful creature! Its eyes shone yellow in the morning light. Its tail streamed behind it like a banner. Where could it be going with such strength of purpose?

Over broken granite, through dead heather, and past a grove of bare-branched rowans, Abby followed the fox. It moved slowly, a red tear trickling over the gray face of the hills. At last it stopped, sniffed the air, and bolted.

"Come back!" cried Abby. She scanned the heather for a glimpse of the fascinating animal. "Come back!" Her voice echoed back to her over the moor, small and empty-sounding. What a ninny she was, shouting for a wild beast to return. If anything, she was driving it away. A red patch on the hillside caught her eye, and she scrambled toward it.

It was not the fox. It was a person. Two people.

The stench of gore filled Abby's nostrils. She turned with a scream of horror. Yet she had to look again. Again she screamed. The third time she looked, she did not turn away. The poor creatures!

The bodies of a man and woman lay before her, the man atop his lover, still joined to her in the act of love. A single musketball had killed them both, shattering the back of the man's

head before plunging into the forehead of the
woman. Her long, yellow hair lay spread out
above her head like straw upon a blanket of
blood.

This passage uses three senses—sight, hearing and smell—
to help the reader visualize this grim incident. The detailed
description of the fox gives us an impression of Abby's curiosity
and her observant nature. The echoing sound of her voice
suggests the vast desolation and loneliness of the moor. The
scent of blood is a strong, immediate image of horror and danger
which sets the reader up for the macabre scene which follows.

The scene itself is rendered in concise, visceral images: dead
bodies joined in the act of love, a shattered head, an implied
bullethole in the forehead, yellow hair like straw on a blanket of
blood. Note that the visceral images are not overdone. There is
just enough imagery to set the scene. The writer's intention was
to tell the reader only enough so that the reader could see the
scene for himself and be drawn into it. Any more such imagery
might have actually revolted the reader and mentally pushed
him right out of the scene.

Knowing when enough imagery is enough is a matter of
practice, but you can generally assume that too little is better
than too much. In F. Scott Fitzgerald's *The Great Gatsby*, just one
mention of one image—that of a cufflink made from a human
molar—is enough to tell us more than we want to know about
the wearer of the cufflink. Note that too much imagery rapidly
turns into "overwriting," which is discussed later.

In your writing, you want to incorporate images of all five
senses. Keep in mind that the strongest imagery seems to be
connected with the sense of smell. Smells are often associated
with childhood experiences—the scent of ripe blueberries, the

stink of cattle, the odor of musty hay in Grandfather's loft, the sweet fragrance of new sheets. Using smell imagery, you have immediate control over the reader's most basic, visceral emotions and reactions. With the right olfactory images, you can easily shock or frighten the reader (the scent of blood), disgust him (vomit), delight him (candy canes), make him feel nostalgic (Papa's cigars), make him hungry (apple pie baking in the oven), or arouse his sexuality (human musk).

Imagery Exercise One

Objective: To use descriptive words and phrases

Part 1

List as many adjectives as you like to describe the following objects. If all five senses apply, try to use all five in your description.

1. a ripe peach
2. a compost pile
3. the beach on a sunny day
4. a blister, cut, scrape, bruise or other small wound
5. a squirt of toothpaste
6. a gift-wrapped Christmas or birthday present
7. antipasto salad
8. a corn muffin, right out of the oven
9. a mountain stream
10. a downtown street corner in a major American city at 8:00 in the morning on a Monday

Part 2

Here are ten sensory descriptions. Write down your guesses as to what is being described. Some descriptions apply to more than one item.

1. transparent, hard, crystalline, brittle, glittering
2. salty, fishy, savory, crunchy, golden
3. pungent, wrinkled, dark red and brown, dry
4. brassy, hard, shiny, smooth; ticking or buzzing, chiming or ringing
5. squishy, earthy, slimy, cool, sucking, chocolate brown
6. squeaking, warm, hand-sized, soft, sweet-smelling
7. small, soft, smooth, pink or red, fragrant

8. jangling, silver, shiny, hard
9. red, copper-scented, wet, warm
10. plopping, drumming, beating; wet, silver, tiny, sweet-scented, transparent

Imagery Exercise Two

Objective: To use sensory description

Read the paragraph below, which describes a person walking in a field of wildflowers. Something seems to be missing…ah, yes! It's sensory description! How do the flowers feel, smell, look? What sounds might be present in that flowery field? How does the sensory experience of the meadow effect the narrator?

Rewrite the paragraph using appropriate sensory imagery to make the meadow come alive for the reader. You may substitute more familiar flowers, if you wish.

> As I stepped out of the shadow of the fir trees, I noticed a meadow in front of me. I had seen pictures of these wildflowers before—Indian paintbrush, sunflowers and Shasta daisies—but I had never walked among them. I eased into the meadow and breathed deeply. As I brushed past the flowers, their petals glided over my hands. How could I have lived so long and not touched wildflowers before? I thought.

Imagery Exercise Three

Objective: To become aware of imagery

Keep an image journal for at least one week. Every day, write at least one description of an object, animal, place or person. Each description may be anywhere from 2 paragraphs to 2 pages long. Try to include as much sensory description as possible to help the reader imagine the subject you are describing. You might think of this brief journal as a sort of "sketchbook" for the writer.

Imagery Exercise Four

Objective: To notice how published authors use imagery

Locate a favorite descriptive passage in a novel or short story of any genre. It should be at least 8 lines long, preferably longer, and make use of sensory description. (The works of D.H. Lawrence, Eudora Welty, Carson McCullers, J.R. Tolkien, Richard Adams, Katherine Anne Porter, Joseph Conrad, E.M. Forster and John Steinbeck are all good literary sources, though of course you may choose any appropriate passage.) List the ways in which these writers use imagery. What senses do the writers appeal to? What sort of phrases and language do they use?

Using Imagery to Define Characters

Sensual images are so powerful that writers sometimes use such imagery to define or delineate the personality of their major characters. The more aware a protagonist is of his senses, the more he will appear to be aware of the world around him. He will therefore be that much more accessible to the reader.

If you have ever read *The Catcher in the Rye* by J.D. Salinger, you know a character who notices many subtle details about other people. Holden Caulfield sees a school official pick his nose (although he is pretending to scratch it); Holden notices the youth of Sunny the prostitute, despite her makeup and worldly attitude...the kindness in the voices of the traveling nuns...the angora sweater of his wealthy, pretty but superficial girlfriend...the delight in the voice of his little sister when he goes to visit her. Holden notices so many sensory details because he is compelled to try to get closer to people in order to find "his place" in their society. Ultimately he fails to do so. His misinterpretation of a physical gesture—a teacher tousling Holden's hair—drives him away from seeking attachment to people.

Imagery Exercise Five

Objective: To show how imagery helps define character

Read the list of characters below. Jot down or think about how each is likely to react to the following: a friendly cat; the ocean; a violent thunderstorm; a dozen cherry tomatoes; a hyacinth in full bloom; a dim room full of shadows. What is it about the physical nature of each item that solicits the response in each individual?

1. A 5-year-old boy
2. A hostage who has spent the past 2 years in captivity
3. A woman who is rapidly losing her eyesight
4. An artist who is struggling to support his art
5. A man who has only a few months to live
6. A space alien who has the same senses as a human but has never before encountered the objects listed above

Cool Down

Novels of all types and genres will benefit from rich, meaningful imagery. Remember, the images must arise naturally from the events of the plot, the personalities of the characters, and the scope of the story, and should not be tacked on merely to "make things more colorful." We have seen far too many writers make the mistake of overwriting—turning what should be an effective description into an overblown passage. The old adage "less is more" frequently applies to the use of images; one solid image does the trick, while three or four will cancel each other out. Remember also to use all five senses in your writing, and suddenly your fictional world will come to life for the reader.

11
Writing Cramps:
Errors to Avoid in Your Writing

*In everything the middle course is best; all things
in excess bring trouble.*

—Plautus

You've just completed the third revision of your 250-page horror novel and are pretty proud of yourself. You decide to take a quick read through it to correct typos, when, to your horror, you find dozens of impish errors grinning back at you from your writing. *How did that stuff get in there?*

Contrivances, clichés, passive constructions, ellipses that

won't quit, an embarrassing racial stereotype, several passages of lyrical fluff that has no purpose at all in the story…what are these things and how did they happen?

These horrid things are "writing cramps" and they can weaken your writing without your knowledge. In reality, they are just common but sneaky errors that should be corrected as soon as you notice them or someone points them out to you. These writing cramps normally attack when the writer is tired, stressed or just working too hard at the business of writing. Cramps are also often the result of being out of point of view, or not crafting a point of view in the first place. Since failure to thoroughly plan the structure of the novel will also result in sloppy errors, a good outline can be a real lifesaver.

In short, any time there is a "crack" in your craft—you're unsure how to proceed; your POV is weak; you push the panic button and reach for the easiest conflict resolution; you take a very large, not-well-calculated risk—the writing cramps are sure to creep into your novel and play havoc with it.

Here is a list of the most common types of writing cramps and how they do their devilish work. They are presented in no particular order.

1. *Contrivances*—A contrivance is anything in your writing which is awkwardly presented or obviously manipulated by the writer to achieve a predetermined, usually predictable result. It is the literary equivalent of watching a science fiction movie and noticing the nylon strings that hold up the model space ship. The reader can see the writer at work, forcing the behavior of characters and the nature of events. *Deus ex machina*—"god from a machine"—is a common contrivance in which a rescuer appears out of nowhere to miraculously save the hero from danger.

2. *Overwriting*—The bane of existence for writers trying to use description, overwriting takes two forms: either too much descriptive prose or too florid descriptive prose. It may be enough to say that your protagonist runs into a forest; probably you don't need an in-depth description of the forest at this point. Perhaps you'd like to describe it as a "dark forest of spruce and cedar." If you describe it as "a dark, sweet-scented, somehow foreboding forest populated by the stark ghosts of blue spruce and the clublike apparitions of ancient cedars," then you've probably said far-r-r too much.

    To curb overwriting, keep in mind that description must have a purpose in your story. It should not be used just to fill in blank space or show off your talent for lyrical writing. Before you use imagery and description, make sure you understand what feeling or information you are trying to get across to the reader. Also, remember that any description must be in a point of view and must be consistent with that character's personality. It's unlikely, for instance, that a forest ranger would come up with the afore-mentioned description of a forest.

3. *Cinematic Point of View*—Yes, we've covered it earlier, but we just can't mention it often enough: Don't view your novel as a movie or screenplay. It is a tremendously distancing technique, and you generally don't want to distance your readers too much from your writing. If you find yourself thinking in terms of close-ups, cuts, foregrounds, backgrounds and pans of landscapes, take a break and rethink your presentation. Get to know your characters better and try to see the events of the novel from their eyes.

4. *Clichés*—Even the best writers embrace this "muscle cramp" now and then. Thus we get "chills running down her spine," a character who "gives up the ghost" or "passes on to his reward" or experiences his heart "leaping into his throat." We also get "as hungry as a bear," "as fierce as a tiger," and "She could swim like a fish." Clichés should be avoided like…well, the plague.

Clichés need not be phrases. The term can also refer to trite, overdone situations or resolutions. Remember the early episodes of *Star Trek*, in which junior officers beamed down to strange planets to investigate unusual events inevitably got killed? Eventually this plot device became a sort of "in joke" with the show's supporters. If your male protagonist is awakened in the morning by a phone call from his wife, avoid the temptation to let the "camera pull back" to reveal a woman in bed with your protagonist. This is trite, tired stuff. Seek the fresh, the original (there's still some of that commodity out there), the innovative twist on an old theme.

The term cliché also applies to characters, as we discussed earlier. Avoid using stock characters—the smothering stage mother; the dull-witted, gorilla-like thug; the fussy, older librarian; the computer-loving, near-sighted nerd who is either a virgin or is always surrounded by women. Try to create realistic, three-dimensional characters who are sympathetic yet perhaps flawed in believable ways.

5. *Gaffes*—These provide entertainment for editors, but gaffes are surely not the sort of thing you want to write. Some examples of unintentionally humorous, bizarre or just plain bad writing we've come across personally:

—The injured falcon ate like a bird.

—Sitting on the window ledge, his arms reached out for her.

—The Indian dropped a pebble into the fisher (fissure) to test its depth.

—Evangeline heard a knocking at her door: THUD THUD THUD.

—"Sit down, Rick," Evans said. He propped his feet on a chair and poured them both a cup of coffee.

—His eyes bounced from curtain to curtain.

—Her fingers turned the key in the ignition.

—She held his eyes with a proud glare.

Body parts, especially eyes, seem to pose a special problem for some writers. When writing about people seeing things, use "sight" verbs such as gazed, stared, looked, saw, glimpsed, scanned, glared, eyed, spied, ogled, and so on. If you like, you might try a sentence such as, "His steady gaze penetrated her resistance." Avoid letting eyes or other body parts do the work of the character.

When in doubt about how a passage sounds, read it aloud. Often writers can hear the errors that they cannot see or automatically correct when reading.

6. *Present tense and tense shifts*—We've mentioned present tense before, but the admonition bears repeating: Don't use present tense unless you feel you must, and try not to use it at all for longer fiction. If you do decide to use present tense, use it consistently throughout your novel. Avoid switching back and forth from present to past tense, which is very confusing to your readers.

7. *Style*—Have you noticed that we have not given style more than a passing reference in this book? That is because we believe style is not something you can learn, nor is style something that is "added" to a manuscript. Master writers such as Katherine Anne Porter and Ernest Hemingway wrote and practiced writing for years in order to develop their distinctive styles. It is probably wrong-headed and ultimately self-defeating to think in terms of writing a piece in a certain "style." The elusive search for style usually ends up in a meeting of Overwriters Anonymous. Try not to be concerned with the style of your writing; style changes and develops at its own pace, based on how often you write and how dedicated you are to learning how to write.

8. *Deliberate confusion*—Some years ago, Italian writer Umberto Ecco admitted that he had intentionally written the first 100 pages of his novel, *The Name of the Rose*, to be confusing. He had thought of those pages as a sort of "penance" for the reader.

    Since you are not a popular, established writer like Umberto Ecco, we strongly recommend that you steer clear of confusing your readers on purpose. It is altogether too easy to do unintentionally. Instead, respect your reader and think in terms of how you can help him understand your writing without insulting his intelligence by explaining it to him. Writers who deliberately try to confuse their readers often think they are being "artistic" or "innovative;" more often than not, they are just being conceited.

9. *Backtracking*—Backtracking occurs when a writer begins to narrate a scene, then inexplicably leaps back to an earlier time, before the scene took place. For ex-

ample: "Bob and Sophie entered the restaurant and were shown to an elegant table by the big picture window. That morning, Bob had called Sophie to ask her out to dinner."

Backtracking is not a flashback, since it is not a memory and is not rendered in a point of view. It is simply a sequencing mistake. To avoid sequencing errors of all sorts, try to render the story chronologically, with the judicious use of flashbacks to highlight prior events.

10. *Episodic structure*—How does your novel progress from one scene to the next? Does it proceed from event to event to event, as if scenes were strung like beads on a string? Or does the reader get a feeling of a bigger picture, that the events are part of a larger circumstance that is propelling the protagonist through the novel? Is there a theme underlying the structure of your work? Some types of novels lend themselves to an episodic structure: Any novel based on a quest (*Lord of the Rings, The Grapes of Wrath, As I Lay Dying*) will naturally move from event to event. Fantasy, science fiction and historical novels are often by nature rather episodic. The key is to make sure each separate event is somehow connected to a larger theme, greater circumstance or encompassing conflict. For instance, in *Lord of the Rings*, the hobbits and their allies experience many adventures, yet their all-consuming task of destroying the ring and preserving order in Middle Earth is always present in their minds.

11. *Putting Theme First*—Having a message or "big picture" in your novel is fine, if not preferable, but theme cannot come first. Theme should arise naturally from the char-

acters, the events and the conflict of the novel. Therefore, you start with your characters, developing and
visualizing them. Then you imagine how you can exert
pressure on them to change. After examining this scenario, you might conclude that it illustrates Man's Inhu-
manity to Man, or The Indestructible Resilience of
Nature, or some other larger theme. But the characters
and events in the novel should not be seen as merely a
means to expressing or giving form to an idea. Such a
decision usually results in a very distant, stiff narration
that is largely devoid of feeling and three-dimensional
characters.

12. *Who is Your Audience?*—It's a good rule of thumb not to
begin to write until you know who you are writing for.
Your mental image of your reader will help determine
what you write and how you write it. For example, you
would not write a young adult western the same way you
write a western trade novel. Vocabulary, pacing, exposition and plotting would all be different for each. One
writer who mentioned "the pungent odor of creosote" in
his young adult fantasy was told to reconsider the
vocabulary of his readers.

   Some facets to keep in mind about your readers
include their age, sex, educational level, cultural background, ethnic background and even their reading hab-
its. If they have read a great deal of science fiction, for
example, they may be more critical of your space opus
than other readers. Thus you will have to "know your
stuff" and do your research in order to please this
demanding audience.

13. *Passive Voice and Passive Constructions*—In general, you
want your writing to be direct and forceful. You want to

avoid "backing into" your writing by writing in the passive voice, or by using passive sentence constructions which shift the emphasis of an action away from the character and place it on the object receiving the action. For example, the following sentence is written in the passive voice: "An arrow was shot by Cadmus, who had seen the wolf attacking Christian." This sentence weakens the drama of the action by making the arrow, not Cadmus, the most important part of the sentence. It sounds to the reader as if the arrow is taking action, when it is really Cadmus who is perceiving the situation and responding to it. To make this an active sentence, as opposed to a passive one, we could rewrite it thus: "Cadmus saw the wolf attacking Christian and shot an arrow at it."

Passive constructions are trickier to avoid. They are not necessarily in the passive voice, but have the same results. Here is an example: "The arrow streaked from Cadmus's bow and flew into the heart of the wolf." Again, why place the emphasis on the inanimate object? It is Cadmus who is taking action, not his equipment. One could write this scene from Cadmus's POV: He sees Christian being attacked. Alternatively, Christian could observe this scene: He sees Cadmus ready the arrow, or he hears the arrow enter the wolf and feels the animal grow limp. (Once again, notice that point of view comes to the rescue here.)

Another aspect of passive writing involves the overuse of -ly adverbs: gladly, quickly, stoically, haltingly, sheepishly, violently and so on. A few here and there are helpful; more than occasional use, however, results in some pretty weak writing.

If you find you are using several -ly adverbs every page, check your verbs. You can probably avoid most adverbs by using stronger verbs. For example, why write "moved quickly" when you can write "ran," "galloped," "rushed," "hurried" or "darted?"

14. …,—, !!!, and ?!—We do not cover grammar in this book because we hope you know grammar already. If you are unsure of standard grammar, take a look at some of the fine grammar books available in your local library or bookstore.

However, one grammar problem is so common among beginning writers that we feel compelled to mention it here. It is the overuse of certain items of punctuation, namely ellipses (…), m-dashes (—), exclamations and question marks (!!! or ???) and the interrobang (?!).

Part of the solution to this problem is simple. Don't use more than one exclamation point or question mark, and use exclamation marks only to punctuate true interjections ("Aha!") or short outbursts ("Get him!"). Don't use exclamations to add emphasis to long statements ("I'm never going back with you again, no matter what you say or do!"). Do not use the interrobang in fiction; that's a journalistic device, usually used in humorous essays.

The answers get a little harder when we move on to ellipses and dashes. As a general rule, use ellipses to indicate stammering, hesitation, interruptions or missing material. For example: "What…what are you doing here, Alan? You're supposed to be…that is…." (Notice that the last ellipsis includes a period at the end of the sentence; hence four dots.) Do not use ellipses to take the place of commas: "When you reach Cygnus 5...which lies in the far reaches of the Tortoise Nebula...you'll receive the rest of your orders."

An m-dash (—) is not the same as a hyphen (-) and should not be indicated by a hyphen. If your keyboard does not have an m-dash, used double hyphens (--) to indicate the dash. M-dashes are long dashes used to interject asides into sentences. "Some of the girls—but by no means all—are terrible flirts." A dash can also be used to take the place of a colon in some cases for emphasis. ("He's got the answer—run!") The dash should not be used when a comma will do. By the way, the m-dash, or em-dash, which got its name in the days of handset type, is the same length as the printer's measure "em," the length of the letter m.

Writing cramps have only one mission: to sabotage your writing and make it less readable and accessible. Therefore, when you are working on a novel, you should take pains to avoid muscle cramps by reading your entire work slowly and carefully at least once during the revision process, preferably aloud to another person. You cannot avoid all writing errors, but you can minimize them.

Time to Hit the Shower

Congratulations! You've gone the distance. You've finished this literary workout, and we hope that, in doing so, you've learned some important things about one of the most strenuous activities on the planet: writing fiction.

You've practiced "getting ready to write" and learned some techniques for improving your powers of observation and creativity. You've learned about the key role characters and point of view play in the development of a novel, and you've sweated through the concept of a plot and several plotting techniques, such as suspense and scene. Setting, tone/voice, narrative, dialogue and imagery should all be familiar terms by now, and you probably recognize cinematic writing, passive writing, and the other muscle cramps that try to knock you out of your Reeboks.

Now you are ready to begin to write a novel. Don't be disappointed or surprised if you find that you need still more exercise in the writing gym. There is no "easy way" to learn to write marketable fiction, nor is there any literary steroid which can aid you in your goal. Practicing your writing skills is the best way to improve your writing. If you can, join writing classes or workshops and learn from the criticism of your peers and mentors. Reading quality fiction will also help your writing.

For more challenging exercises and the next step in the program, read our second book in this series, *Writing Aerobics II: Exercises for the Intermediate Writer.*

Once again, congratulations. Now go hit the shower.